The Party System and the Corruption of Parliament

By
Ben Greene

MAPLE
PUBLISHERS

The Party System and the Corruption of Parliament

Author: Ben Greene

Copyright © Ben Greene (2023)

The right of Ben Greene to be identified as author of this work has been asserted by the author in accordance with section 77 and 78 of the Copyright, Designs and Patents Act 1988.

First Published in 2023

ISBN 978-1-915796-19-6 (Paperback)
        978-1-915796-22-6 (E-Book)

Book Cover Design and Layout by:
        Maple Publishers
        www.maplepublishers.com

Published by:
        Maple Publishers
        Fairbourne Drive, Atterbury,
        Milton Keynes,
        MK10 9RG, UK
        www.maplepublishers.com

A CIP catalogue record for this title is available from the British Library.

FOREWORD

In this work on the English Constitution by Ben Greene, Greene scrutinises and challenges the ideas of A. V. Dicey, the celebrated 19th-century legal scholar. It was Dicey who, with his theories of parliamentary sovereignty, attempted to give juristic validity to the parliamentary processes that had emerged after the 2nd Reform Act of 1867. Although Dicey had no authority to rule on such matters, his theories, first published in 1885, received much acclaim and, in particular, served as a boon to the political establishment of the day. But, as time wore on, Greene notes, Dicey increasingly commented on inadequacies in the system — a system he was a sole party in endorsing — to deliver expected or even satisfactory results. He also may have become aware of inconsistencies in his work. Despite these concerns, Dicey retracted none of his theories.

The Second Reform Act, at the time of its introduction, gave the promise of ushering in a new democratic age. But, according to Greene, changes to the internal structures within political parties, occurring contemporaneously with the Reform Act worked in the background to undermine the intention behind the Act and even succeeded in reducing the already established level of political representation. Greene devotes nearly a whole chapter to chronicling these changes.

The forces that came into being after the 2nd Reform Act built themselves on those that followed the 1st Reform Act of 1832. This latter Act had brought Benthamite influence to power, and it was under this influence, Greene points out, that the whole tenor and tone of English Law changed.

To throw some light on the Benthamite mindset, Greene draws parallels with the physiocratic school of economic thought from 18th century France. It was from this group that Benthamites derived many ideas and took many of their ideological cues. After examining France's situation regarding the period before its revolution, Greene identifies two factors that generally go unnoticed by historians. These are highly noteworthy because, when the time came, in the turmoil that followed the French Revolution, they were instrumental in allowing the political despotisms, highly characteristic of the Old Regime, to pass, unnoticed and unchallenged, into the system that was to replace it.

Firstly, the French Enlightenment itself. Despite the impact enlightenment philosophers made on the intellectual landscape of the day, as Greene explains, it had remained little more than intellectual activity. While it was a relatively easy step to reject the doctrine of divine right, it was an entirely different matter to come to grips with one of the latter's most problematic aspects — the Lex Regia. Several centuries had separated the French nation from the knowledge and practicalities of common law that alone might have made this possible. Lex Regia, a legalised code of political tyranny, Greene continues, was a corrupted form of Roman Civil Law that had, after a hiatus of a millennium, reappeared to embed itself in the politico-legal codes of Renaissance Europe.

Secondly, at this juncture of history, on the cusp of the industrial revolution, a new dynamic, not entirely consistent with enlightenment aspirations, was invisibly at work. One very noticeable feature of political economy, the tenets of which both Benthamites and Physiocrats adhered to with a religious-like zeal, is a continuous fluctuation of fortune. And Greene makes a critical point here; such a system, introduced to a nation in which a significantly large part of the population possesses no economic buffer to withstand such fluctuation, would require this system to be maintained on the principles of coercion. Greene asserts it was to serve such a dynamic in Britain, under the guise of counter-coercion, that the radical politics of the age of progress and reform came into being.

The Benthamites talked of liberty and equality and, in so doing, could claim Enlightenment credentials. However, they tended to see progress in materialistic terms only, where progress was to be guided by principles based on the pursuit of self-interest. What this boiled down to on an individual level was the pursuit of profit, regardless of consequence. This last point, Greene explains, formed the basis of their idea of liberty. And equality to them, in Greene's estimation, would mean nothing more than an equality of conditions, a uniformity of circumstance, in which they could exert the iron grip of their will with greater ease and in which, conveniently, huge inequalities might go unnoticed. Like the Physiocrats before them, Benthamite Utilitarians, whatever else they considered themselves to be, saw themselves as the social masters of the new industrial age. Impassioned by what they believed to be the superiority of their ideas and seeking to impose their ideology on others, they regarded any obstacle in their path as an unconscionable tyranny. Such an obstacle they saw in the English Constitution and the common laws upon which it based itself. The Constitution, for instance, lacked inherent powers of coercion. The three branches of government each exercised supremacy in their respective spheres of expertise, but no one branch possessed any authority to dictate to either of the other two.

To overcome this hurdle, the Benthamites set about propagating the doctrine, based on a falsehood, that the English Constitution was no other than a long protracted historical process of struggle against a despotic monarchy — a process in which they represented the finest, if not final, expression. And it was on this confabulation that the premise of the radical mindset rested. The inherent duplicity of this position did not go unnoticed — Greene draws attention to the Chartist movement here—but the political developments set in motion by this new doctrine also led to a prolonged process of obfuscation. This latter which could be described as Orwellian, disguised what would become, under growing Benthamite control, little more than political dictatorship. The ideas of the legal scholar John Austin, entirely inappropriate to the United Kingdom Legislature, were also adopted and promoted. Through this same process, too, Britain's textbooks would come to be rewritten so as to harmonise with the radical temper of the time. And it was upon this disinformation that nearly two centuries of misinformation have come to be based. Using a sometimes-repetitive manner to drive his point home and writing in a proud and patriotic tone, which with good reason, he feels perfectly justified in using, Greene brushes aside all the accumulated clutter of misconception. And, taking his readers through the twists and turns of history, and drawing upon centuries of statute and debate, brings the English Constitution suddenly and coherently to life.

Long before the age of democracy had dawned, the English had stumbled upon a priceless secret in their empirically based pursuit of greater liberty. The key to this secret lay in the separation of the governing powers of the ruler. And with this came the ability to tame and subdue one of the most dangerous forces known to humankind — the arbitrary power of the state. It is this wisdom with which Its Constitution deals that modern Britain, under the influence of contemporary politics, has cast by the wayside.

The age of progress and reform came and went. In its wake, the toxic political circuitry set up to serve the ideological dictates of the period did not pass with it but became the platform on which the political party system was to base its relentless dominion over Britain's population.

Steven Biezanek

Petts Wood, Kent 2022

INTRODUCTION TO AUTHOR

Ben Greene, Quaker, pacifist, and humanitarian was born in Santos, Brazil, in 1901. When he was nine, his family moved to England, where Greene continued his education. The First World War ended shortly before his seventeenth birthday, and due to a combination of personal conviction and family influences, he had, by this time, become a pacifist. Studying at Oxford, Greene adopted the Quaker religion in rejection of organised Christianity, which in his mind, had morally failed humanity through its inability to prevent or alleviate any of the horrors of the Great War.

During this period, Greene put himself forward as a volunteer to work in the much-needed relief programs the Society of Friends had set up in post-war Europe. This work took him to Germany and, later, war-torn, and famine-ravaged Russia. The situation in Germany opened Greene's eyes to the smouldering widespread resentment against the terms of the Versailles Treaty and the new democratic German Republic that had accepted them. Greene, like others, had hoped that the aftermath of the war would usher in a lasting period of peace and prosperity. But he came quickly to realise that without any revision to any of the terms of the Versailles Treaty, these hopes might never materialise and that there were grave dangers that another war might, eventually, break out.

It was a combination of this desire to campaign for some revision of the Treaty and a desire to promote social justice in post-war Britain that led Greene to join the Labour Party. During the 1924 Labour Government, he served as Private Secretary to Ramsey MacDonald and later, at different times, stood, albeit unsuccessfully, as a Labour candidate for the Hull and Gravesend constituencies. After noticing a lack of transparency in the Labour Party's internal structure, he attempted to infuse a more democratic element into this by setting up the Constituency Parties Movement. How successful this was is unclear because when, at a later date, the Labour National Executive told him he would be among those elected to join its ranks, even before the voting had started, he rejected the offer in disgust. This rejection was to mark the beginning of a strained relationship with senior Labour figures. This souring and continuing disagreement with them over the Versailles Treaty issue would lead to a rift that would eventually result in Greene resigning from the Labour

Party in 1938. And when the time came, this hardening of arteries meant Greene would stand isolated and vulnerable with few friends, if not enemies, in influential places.

As the 1930s progressed, Greene had turned some of his attention to helping to advocate for the welfare of refugees arriving, in increasing numbers, on our shores from Nazi Germany. He also acted, at this time, as Deputy Returning Officer for the League of Nations plebiscite in the Saar region. On the second visit to the area in this capacity — the Jewish situation in Germany, by this time, becoming one of increasing international concern — the Quakers asked Greene to investigate specific events that had been reported in the British press. While so doing, he saw, first-hand, the desperate plight of the Jewish community and quickly set about developing a plan for a coordinated relief effort involving the Red Cross, the Quakers, and various Catholic and Protestant organisations. This initiative would combine immediate financial relief alongside an organised system of emigration. The idea, needless to say, was hugely welcomed within the Jewish community in Germany. His work regarding the Saar Plebiscite had already given him points of contact within the German Government. At first, no one in that quarter would cooperate. Still, Greene persevered by explaining that, as a Quaker, his motivation was purely humanitarian and non-political and that he had campaigned for many years, on Germany's behalf, over the issue of the Versailles Treaty. This approach finally worked, and the German authorities invited him to return shortly to discuss the scheme details.

However, while back in Britain, Greene encountered a setback with this plan. The Bank of England had started at this time to disallow currency transfers across the German border amidst heightening international tensions. This new development threw up a severe obstacle to Geene's plan, which would have relied on the evacuees having money in their own hands to initiate their exodus. By this time, because of Nazi policy, Germany had almost wholly excluded the Jewish community from participating in economic activity, and all who remained were in desperate financial plight. Try as he might persuade them, Greene could not get the Bank to back down on this issue regardless of the worthiness of the cause he was espousing. Disappointed with this but refusing to give up hope, he kept his channels with the German authorities open until the last permissible minute.

World War 2, when it broke, saw an MI5 under increasing pressure to identify and detain anyone whose loyalty to the nation might be suspect. It was in this maelstrom of counterespionage activity that Greene fell prey to an ambitious and rising in importance MI5 officer under the name of Maxwell Knight.

Anthony Masters, in his biography of Knight, (*The Man who was M*, Basil Blackwell, 1984) discusses the details of the circumstances leading up to Greene's internment. According to Masters, certain aspects of Knight's character and personality — Knight was an otherwise highly talented individual — contributed to his failure to recognise the absolute difference in mindset between Greene and himself. Knight still clung to vague but boyish romantic notions about the glories of war as portrayed in adventure books. He had seen none of the genuine horrors of war that action in battle provides, despite having served in the Royal Naval Reserve in the last year of the Great War. On the other hand, in his youth as a relief agency worker, Greene would have witnessed many of these horrors almost first-hand. Before WW2 Greene had been focusing his energies on an ambitious plan to rescue those suffering in Germany from Nazi policies. In true Quaker tradition, he had, not without some success, exercised the utmost diplomacy and the strict neutrality required when dealing with the Nazi authorities. Obstacles he encountered were not down to any shortfall as a Quaker but lay in developments outside Germany. These subtleties were lost on Knight. In his eager quest for scalps, he robotically eyed Greene's stance of neutrality with suspicion and viewed him as a legitimate target. This failure of Knight to see what was clear to many others would lead to Greene's internment under Section 18B and his own downfall—according to Masters, after the affair, the Government was never to trust Knight's judgement again fully. After becoming increasingly frustrated with unfruitful attempts to either incriminate Greene or reduce his influence within the community by slurring his name, Knight resorted to the use of false witness.

Greene may have been the only internee detained under Section 18B who, eventually, received a list of reasons for why he had been arrested. When he did receive these, he was able to quickly refute all charges except, that is, the one that used false witness. However, Knight had mishandled this, and the Greene family solicitor skilfully cornered the individual Knight had used as an agent and obtained a signed retraction. With this retraction the Government ordered Greene to be released from Brixton Prison. However, this new development may well have been a cause of uneasiness for Knight. The private detective agency, employed by the Greene family to investigate the circumstances around Greene's detention, had already linked Knight with the individual concerned — the latter had even been named in debate in the House of Lords — although no connection to a government agency had yet been made. There remained, however, the danger of a hugely embarrassing scandal, and Greene had already begun proceedings against the Government for false imprisonment at Law.

At this point, an entirely new document, alleged in Masters' book as a forgery, suddenly appeared in Greene's file at M.I.5. The Home Office no doubt welcomed the cover provided by this new addition in the light of Greene's legal action. But they also may have possibly sensed its dubious provenance and concluded that the less public scrutiny it received, the better. Greene certainly would have wasted no time in challenging it. In any event, the Government cited the Official Secrets Act, resulting in Greene not having access to all the details necessary for a successful action in court. Thus, his attempt to gain legal redress failed. One consequence of this failure was that it conveniently removed legal obstacles to falsely slurring Greene as an individual with possible enemy fascist sympathies — an expedient that gave Knight much needed cover. This slur continues to remain, as any online search will confirm. The irony was that Greene, although a liberal at heart, was the only left-wing-leaning individual — to anyone's knowledge — to have been interned under section 18B during the Second World War.

His health, in ruins, after two years in Brixton Prison, Greene withdrew from public life to take care of the family business. However, service to his country and others was part of his nature. And in his cell, a prisoner of the state, he had begun the work of authoring this book. — a book that unravels the intricacies of the English Constitution, a blueprint for freedom for his and future generations. He passed away in 1978.

*To avoid numerous footnotes in the text, please note that Greene writes from around the middle three decades of the 20th Century.

Contents

Introduction

It is now one hundred years since the modern system of disciplined and caucus-controlled parties founded by Joseph Chamberlain and Benjamin Disraeli established its domination over the elected membership of the British Parliament. This has resulted in the Party Cabinet replacing Parliament as the supreme authority of the British nation.

If this usurpation of Parliamentary supremacy by the Party Cabinet stands confirmed, then we face the final end of our Parliamentary constitution of law and government.

The English Parliamentary Constitution was the greatest achievement in the art of free and strong government in the history of civilised mankind. No other system of Government can show such a record of consistent veneration from those subject to its authority.

The enduring strength and stability of the English Parliamentary constitution, through all the centuries of its existence, arose from the fact that it was founded in the law of the land, which was derived solely from the consent of her people. All authority was bounded by this law which no ruler could change nor disregard but which he was bound to administer. Such was the meaning of the Rule of Law in England.

This concept of English law and government stood in direct contrast to that established in all the other communities of the West, where following the reception of the revived Roman Civil code, the doctrine was enforced that the people had unconditionally surrendered their rights and liberties into the hands of their rulers, whose will and command was the source of law, but by which these rulers themselves could not be bound. In other words, the Roman Civil Code established a lawless sovereignty as the basis of law and Government, and provided the legal condition for every tyranny, despotism and dictatorship which has afflicted the western world since the close of the Middle Ages.

The English people alone of all the western communities resisted the reception of the Roman Civil code, and rejected the lawless sovereignty it postulated. Instead, the English retained their native laws on which the great Common Law of England was founded. The people of England have thus never, in fact or fiction, conditionally or unconditionally, by conquest or by grant surrendered their rights and liberties; and to preserve and maintain them remains the fundamental principle of the English constitution.

With Parliament at its central core, this system of law and government established the practical mechanism of a legal democracy by means of which the people, through the jury system, administered their own law, and by direct representation in the House of Commons controlled their own government. As Sir Lewis Namier, the historian pointed out; -

> "In England since the disappearance of villeinage none of the three elements of democracy was ever altogether absent. At the root of English democracy lies the right of every man to life, liberty and property. To secure it was the first purpose of self government; of trial by jury and taxation by consent. The individual rights of the free-born Englishman have retained their place in the political Code of the nation, but in time they have come to be considered sufficiently secure, not to require constant jealous watching."

(Conflict - Studies in contemporary history. Page187)

With the establishment of the modern militarised Party system in the last hundred years, this great heritage of English law and government has been undermined by the rejection of any concept of law as derived from the consent of the people. Instead, it postulates the modern doctrine of the sovereignty of Parliament under which all law is derived solely from the will and command of Parliament, now controlled by the Party system itself.

The immediate consequence of the doctrine of Parliamentary sovereignty is the total nullification of all constitutional law by which the legal supremacy of Parliament is established. It further nullifies the constitutional rights and liberties of every free-born Englishman* on which the English Parliamentary constitution was founded.

* The term Englishman is an outdated expression for any British person

Under the Party cabinet system with its doctrine of Parliamentary sovereignty what is constitutional in law can now be unconstitutional in practice and the practices of the party system must now be accepted as constitutional however flagrantly illegal. The rule of law now no longer pertains in England as far as government authority is concerned.

The party cabinet has no legal or constitutional standing and is a secret entity of whose activities nothing is allowed to be known.

Of the party system itself, we know little or nothing. What we do know is that it consists of private unincorporated oligarchical associations under no legal or public control. Of the management and activities of these associations we know little or nothing. We know little or nothing of the rules governing these associations, though these now represent the basis of national authority. We do not know under what influences these parties act. We have little or no information as to the sources from which the parties derive their huge financial requirements, the sources of which must play a decisive part in Party direction. We are ignorant of how this finance is expended.

The power of the party cabinet is now so absolute in all matters political that no authority, however legal, can be claimed or exercised except through the party system itself. So absolute is the power of the Party system that anyone acting on its behalf enjoys complete immunity from personal responsibility. However disastrous the consequences of any policy may be no one is held personally accountable; no matter how disgraceful an event may prove, no matter how costly to the nation in life and treasure, no one is personally culpable. We have today an immense civil service wielding dictatorial powers in many vital departments of our national and personal life which is totally exempt from any constitutional responsibility to Parliament for the use or misuse of the power it exercises. Between it and Parliament stand a screen of professional Party politicians in the highest positions who accept a purely fictional responsibility to a parliament under their absolute control and then only collectively.

The party system has not only engrossed the whole authority of the nation into its own hands, but can successfully prevent the influence of any shade of opinion or the demand for the redress of grievance in Parliament; it permits only its own policy to be given effective expression.

The consequences of a century of Party cabinet government have been catastrophic.

Executive government is probably the most decisive factor in the development of national destiny and welfare. The final test of every political system is its capacity to provide those conditions in which the highest levels of administrative efficiency can be achieved, and in which statesmanship can pursue national policy determined solely by national considerations from generation to generation.

These were the conditions which the English Parliamentary constitution provided to a degree which existed nowhere else and is the reason for English achievement in all fields of endeavour.

Under our Parliamentary constitution we became the most powerful nation in the world; we became the workshop of the world and were the great custodians of civil and political liberty. Since the rise of the Party Cabinet system have we retained our strength? Are we still the nation of the free? Have we succeeded in achieving unity at home? Has the Party Cabinet system allowed us to take advantage of the material resources which were laid at our feet and which with our command of the seas we could have so easily developed? No nation has ever received such a rich heritage as ours, nor presented with such opportunities of mechanical and scientific progress in developing such an inheritance. But what have we done with all this? We played politics to such an extent that our Party leadership is now seeking salvation by submerging our national identity with other nations with which we have no common heritage and whose political systems have shown a chronic instability even greater than our own. Clearly, Party politics has led us into political bankruptcy and national degradation. It has led to the ruin and disintegration of our social and industrial relations. It has led us to the very verge of national extinction. As one Cabinet Minister has complacently put it:-

> "Britain is now a medium sized power whose security depends on NATO, whose economic future may lie within the expanded European Market, whose prosperity is conditioned by the world monetary system and whose industrial future is being partly shaped by huge international companies with headquarters in Detroit, Eindhoven and Tokyo."
>
> (Anthony Wedgewood Benn, Daily Express, 20th November 1969)

To such impotence has the party system by its corruption of Parliament reduced in a hundred years a nation which till then was the greatest, industrial, commercial, and financial power in the history of human civilisation.

The sole justification of the Party Cabinet system is its claim that it marks the supreme development of the historic Parliamentary constitution in the establishment of Parliamentary Government as the constitutional basis of a political democracy. It is by virtue of this claim that all the new democracies, which have emerged in the last hundred years, except those in the South American republics, have followed British example in establishing their own form of parliamentary government. But Parliamentary Government is not the fulfilment of English Constitutional development, but its total negation.

Two hundred years ago, in "Present Discontents," Edmund Burke warned that:-

> "Whenever Parliament is persuaded to assume the offices of executive government, it will lose all the confidence, love and veneration which it has ever enjoyed whilst it was supposed to be the corrective and control on the acting power of the state. This would be the event though its conduct in such a perversion of its functions would be tolerable, just and moderate; but if it should be iniquitous, violent, full of passion and full of action, it would be considered as the most intolerable of all modes of tyranny."

These predictions of Burke have been confirmed by the establishment of Parliamentary Government in the last hundred years.

No one has played a more decisive part in giving Parliamentary Government a constitutional form than A.V. Dicey who, as Professor of English Law at the University of Oxford published "Lectures Introductory to the study of the law of the Constitution," now generally referred to as Dicey's "Law of the Constitution." This work, since its first publication in 1885 has been accepted as the standard authority for the doctrine of Parliamentary Sovereignty, which provided the legal basis of Parliamentary Government. In 1914 before the outbreak of the first world war, Dicey recorded in his introduction to the eighth edition of his work that:

"During forty years, faith in Parliamentary Government
has suffered an extraordinary decline or, as some would
say, a temporary eclipse. This change is visible in every
civilised country."

This loss of faith was no temporary phenomenon. Professor Wade, in his introduction to the Tenth Edition of the same work which appeared in 1960 remarked that:-

"It is undeniable that Parliament has suffered in the eyes
of the public a loss of prestige in the last seventy years...
It must not be forgotten that there can be no check upon
the unscrupulous use of power by a Government which
finds itself in command of a majority in the House
of Commons."

The latest confirmation of Burke's predictions is given with the authority of the Lord Chancellor in the Conservative Party Government. Lord Hailsham is an outspoken believer in Parliamentary Government, which he insists, is the perfection of Parliamentary Democracy. Yet Lord Hailsham declared that:-

"It is the parliamentary majority that has the potential
for tyranny. The thing that courts can't protect you
against is Parliament - the traditional protector of our
liberties. But Parliament is constantly making mistakes
and could, in theory become the most oppressive
instrument in the world..."

(Sunday Times 19th July 1970)

The potential for tyranny confirms the total corruption of Parliamentary authority. This arises from the Party System by which the parliamentary majority is organised and controlled, and by which the Party Cabinet has been established as the supreme authority of the nation.

In England, it was ever axiomatic that any manifestation of despotism and arbitrary power was lawless and therefore destructive of the Rule of Law. By this single standard, the exercise of any authority was judged and if lawless was resisted to the death, whether the authority be that of kings, or popes, or even Parliament itself for the Cromwellian Parliaments of the 17th century stand condemned as lawless to this day. In the last hundred years by the doctrine of Parliamentary sovereignty, Parliament is now the instrument of the lawless and arbitrary power of the party cabinet by which it is controlled. Such a Parliament is therefore incapable of supporting or maintaining the Rule of Law in England. This has been apparent to many serious observers ever since the establishment of the Party Cabinet as the supreme authority of the British nation. Among these we have the testimony of no less an authority than A.V. Dicey himself. It was solely upon his work "Law of the Constitution" that the doctrine of Parliamentary sovereignty was received, and it is solely on this doctrine that the party cabinet now depends. Before the wars of this century and their aftermath beclouded the constitutional issues, Dicey declared in 1914:-

> "The ancient veneration for the rule of law has in England suffered during the last thirty years a marked decline. The truth of this assertion is proved by actual legislation, by the existence in some classes of a certain distrust both of the law and the judges and by some marked tendency towards the use of lawless methods for the attainment of social and political ends..."

And Dicey concluded:-

> "The justification of lawlessness is in England suggested if not caused by the misdevelopment of Party Government. The rule of Party cannot be permanently identified with the authority of the nation or with the dictates of patriotism. This fact has in recent days become so patent that eminent thinkers are to be found who certainly use language which implies that the authority or sovereignty of the nation or even the conception of the national will is a sort of political or metaphysical fiction which wise men will do well to discard."

There is, for us, only one alternative to the Rule of Party and that is the Rule of Law which in England rests upon the supremacy of a legally constituted Parliament. What this means is now lost to us. Today we are unable to distinguish between such opposite concepts as Parliamentary supremacy and Parliamentary sovereignty, between the consent of the people and the will of the people or between constitutional law and the constitutional lawlessness of the so-called conventions of the constitution. This is no call to put the clock back. It was Coke in the reign of Elizabeth I who likened Parliament to the workings of a clock. This Parliamentary clock has been made into a manipulated instrument of outside interests. What we need today is to restore the workings of this clocklike mechanism of our Parliamentary heritage. Then by lawful and legal process, adjust our constitutional heritage to the requirements of our modern age.

The Party System In Britain

The most enduring consequence of French Revolutionary ideology is the concept of political party organisation as the basis of government. It is this concept which the Benthamite movement established in England after the Parliamentary Reform act of 1832.

The novelty of Party in our Parliamentary Constitution can be gauged from the remark of Sir Lewis Namier in his Romanes lecture of 1952 "The Monarchy and the Party system" when he said:-

> "In 1761, not one parliamentary election was determined by Party, and in 1951, not one constituency returned a non-party member."

One of the most remarkable and significant features of the party system is that there has never been a theoretical exposition of it as a basis of free government. In all the vast literature on the science and theory of government, few authorities have been discovered by the parties themselves on which they are able to place any reliance. One of these is Edmund Burke, who declared:-

> "Party is a body of men united for promoting by their joint endeavours the national interest upon some particular principle in which they are all agreed."
>
> (The works of Edmund Burke, World Classics, LXXXI, Vol. 2, p. 82)

It would, however, be an unwarrantable distortion of Burke's beliefs to claim that he thus gave his approval to any kind of political party association. In the same part of the "Present Discontents" from which the above extract is derived, he goes on to say:-

> "In order to throw an odium on political connection, these politicians suppose it a necessary incident to it

that you are blindly to follow the opinion of your party, when in direct opposition to your own clear ideas, a degree of servitude that no worthy man could bear the thought of submitting to; and such as I believe no connection (except some court factions) ever could be so senselessly tyrannical as to impose."

(Vol. 2. P. 84)

The truth is, indeed, the very opposite of what the party interest would like us to believe, for no one has spoken in more condemnatory terms of party government than Burke himself. In his "Vindication of Natural Society," he wrote;-

"The great instrument of all these changes and what infuses peculiar venom into them is Party. It is of no consequence what the principles of any party or what their pretensions are; the spirit which actuates is the same, the spirit of ambition, of self-interest, of oppression and treachery. The spirit entirely reverses all the principles which a benevolent nature has erected within us; all honesty, all equal justice and even the ties of natural society, the natural affections. In a word, we have all seen...we have some of us *felt* such oppression from party Government as no other tyranny can parallel."

(Vol. 1, p. 16)

The leaders of our modern democracy have warned us against the dangers of party. Lord Brougham, who was one of the chief sponsors of the Reform Bill of 1832, had no hesitation in denouncing the falsity and hypocrisy of party claims and their anti-democratic efforts. In his long essay "The Effects of Party", he gives us a detailed, albeit wordy, account of the party system in practice, and he shows that the party in opposition will always oppose the government even on an issue where all their traditions would indicate the reverse. His conclusion is that, whereas Burke had given principle as the sole justification for party association, it is in fact, only interest that compels them to manufacture "principles" often on the spur of the moment to gain the fruits of office. He also makes it clear that the party and its "policy" is imposed on its members, and thus the parties form an effective barrier between the people and their government. (Statesmen of the time of George III, p. 298)

Walter Bagehot, in the "English Constitution," had no illusion as to the nature of party government. He declared:-

> "The only mode by which a cohesive majority and a lasting administration can be upheld in a Parliamentary Government is party organisation, but that organisation itself tends to aggravate party violence and party animosity. It is in substance subjecting the whole nation to a rule of a section of the nation, selected because of its speciality. Parliamentary government is, in its essence, a sectional government."
>
> (Page 204)

John Stuart Mill, in his "Representative Government", gives a party system no part whatever as an organ of democracy, but on the contrary, in so far as he deals with party at all, he aims to minimise and reduce its effect.

Coming to more modern times, we have Lord Bryce, whose writings on democracy were classics of their times. In his preface to Ostrogorski's "Democracy and the Organisation of Political Parties", he wrote:-

> "Once the business of organisation is entered upon, each party has the strongest motive for endeavouring to make its system effective, and to form its adherents into disciplined battalions. But this carries the community still further from the democratic ideal of the intelligent independence of the individual voter, an ideal far removed from the actualities of any state. Organisation and discipline mean the command of the leader, the subordination and obedience of the rank and file; and they mean also the growth of the party spirit, which is in itself irrational, impelling men to vote from considerations which have little to do with love of truth or sense of justice. These are deviations from the democratic ideal which are bad enough and if the

motive of pecuniary advantage is added...the state of things will become still worse."

(Preface, p. XLV)

Only one serious attempt has been made to extol the party system as an instrument of government, and that was by Professor G. M. Trevelyan O.M., the historian, in his Romanes lecture of 1926 under the title of "The Two Party System in England". In this lecture, Trevelyan never examined the modern party system - did not even approach within fifty years of the Reform Act of 1832. He deplored that there were:-

> "...so few serious historical works of our party system, seeing how great a place party held in the growth of our Parliamentary and Cabinet Government."

(An autobiography and other essays, p. 183)

He told us further:-

> "It was the function of this old England, first of all great nations, to show that efficiency could be combined with freedom. Till the defeat of the Grand Monarch of France at La Hogue, Blenheim and Ramillies, it had generally been assumed that countries had to choose between power and safety on one side and liberty on the other."

(Ibid., p. 186)

Is this really true? Does not our whole constitutional system show that liberty founded in law is the foundation of national power? And is it true that many devices which had to be employed included:-

> "This strange one of the party system, the unwritten law underlying the new Parliamentary order of things in England."

(Ibid., p. 187)

In his "History of England." Lord Macaulay has given a completely different picture of the political conditions of this period. It is not possible to quote in full his masterly picture of the cynical party politician, but his conclusion points to the same period to which Professor Trevelyan referred:-

> "Among the politicians who, from the Restoration to the Accession of the House of Hanover, were at the head of the great parties of the state, few can be named whose reputation is not stained by what in our age would be called gross perfidy and corruption. It is scarce an exaggeration to say that the most unprincipled public men who have taken part in affairs within our memory would, if tried by the standard fashionable during the latter part of the seventeenth century, deserve to be regarded as scrupulous and disinterested."

(Page 48)

Can this picture be associated with "efficiency combined with freedom?" If this is not a true picture of the party politician who established this "unwritten" law of our new order, it is indeed tragic that Professor Trevelyan did not use his great historic gifts to correct these devastating conclusions to which his great uncle had come and to give us instead a true history, the absence of which he so deplored.

Till 1832 political parties were loose Parliamentary associations of aristocratic connection. After the Reform Act, political party organisation was extended to the constituencies to enrol the newly enfranchised voters. The organisation of political opinion through the parties reached full development at the time of the second reform act of 1867.

Sir Lewis Namier pointed out in his Romanes Lecture of 1952, "The Monarchy and the Party System":-

> "Nineteenth century historians now seem agreed in deferring the full emergence of the modern party till after the second Reform Bill. What preceded it were intermediate forms which should not be treated anachronistically in terms of a later age."

(Personalities and Power, p. 14)

At the time of the second reform Act, the two main parties were the Liberals and the Conservatives. Gladstone was the virtual leader of the Liberal Party, which had, in its Radical wing, a very pronounced profession of democracy derived from French Revolutionary ideology. After the passing of the second Reform Act, the Liberal Constituency associations for the organisation of the new voters rapidly established themselves quite independently of the Central Office of the Parliamentary party under the control of the party managers who maintained a loose discipline of the Liberal members of Parliament under the party whips. These local associations went further and built up a series of independent regional associations for mutual assistance and government. Each area tended to follow a line of its own, based upon different conceptions of democratic requirements. The most remarkable of these was the Liberal Federation, which Joseph Chamberlain built up in the Birmingham area on the principle of a democracy based on majority rule to the fullest extent of even eliminating any form of minority representation which the Reform Act itself had made possible. The essential principle of the Caucus (as the Birmingham system became known) was to apply this iron principle of majority rule to the organisation of the Party itself so that, once a decision had been reached, the minority had to accept the decision as their own. The trick in this system lay in the ward organisation as the basis of Party membership. As the majority of party members are interested in national issues, ward politics was a matter of little attraction, with the result that attendance at ward meetings was neglected. The only person who might be interested in a general way in ward politics is either a municipal politician or a man who aspires to be a machine politician. He would attend his ward meetings, so that he might be sent as a delegate to the central committee of the city or borough. His voting strength is based upon the membership of his ward. A case could easily arise where a ward party with a membership of over 600 persons, of whom perhaps not more than six would attend the ward meeting called in due accordance with the rules. The delegate to the central committee is appointed by the six, but he carries with him over 600 votes. It is on such voting that the iron law of "majority rule" would be based. For certain types of character, there is nothing more enjoyable than the wire-pulling and manipulation in the packing of ward committees which such a system of democracy provided, and which carry such a wide field of influence in party affairs.

Such persons may never appear before the public eye, and yet the whole political organisation can be manipulated by them. Men with some intelligence choose the high road in preferment as party candidates.

They may have the show and they may even have a little influence if elected; but they are selected and therefore controlled by the party machine, and the party machine is controlled by the ward politician, who is usually a henchman of the association managers. It is such a system which Chamberlain established. Birmingham Liberals were pledged to the decisions of the Federation, arrived at by means they thought they understood, but which the Federation managers understood even better.

The sole purpose of such political machines was to win elections with candidates under control. Not only were liberal voters told how to vote, but members, when elected, were also told how to vote. The revolutionary constitutional implications can best be judged by the expressions of contemporary opinion when the new form of machine politics was first introduced. There are several historic cases of the forlorn fight which Liberal members of Parliament waged against the Caucus when it was established in their constituencies. The case of Dewsbury is perhaps the most instructive, for the sitting member argued his case in a letter published in "The Times".

This member had been elected for Dewsbury on two or three occasions as a Liberal on his own professions. He had not only Conservative but Liberal opponents as well, and his success on each occasion would indicate that he had the confidence of the electors. He had supported the reform act of 1867. On 20th September 1878, there was addressed to this Member a letter in the following terms:-

> "As secretary of the meeting of the Executive of the Dewsbury Parliamentary Borough Joint Liberal Association on the Birmingham plan (i.e. the Caucus) held on Monday evening last, I have to inform you that you were nominated as a candidate. On behalf of the Association may I ask you whether you will allow your name to be proposed at the General Committee meeting to be held on Tuesday 30th instant, and if so, whether you will abide by the decision of the Association."
>
> (The Times 6th October 1879)

To this communication, the sitting member for Dewsbury gave a long reply, and the following extracts will show the constitutional revolution implied in the above letter, which today would be accepted as a matter of course. The member wrote:-

> " In reply to your letter of 20th ultimo, I have now to say that if the Association of their own free will determine to give me their support as the Liberal candidate at the next election, I shall be much gratified, for I believe it would be the certain means of bringing about that union of the Liberal Party in the borough, which is our common object and desire to secure. But I cannot accept the condition proposed, that if nominated as a candidate, I will abide by the decision of the Association. I cannot be a party of any proceedings that would stand between a candidate and the free choice of the constituency. I object to it as an infringement of the electoral freedom of the constituency. It would virtually transfer from them the whole electoral power of the borough, so far at least as the Liberal electors are concerned, to the association or its committee. It would, in effect, restore the old system of nomination boroughs. Large constituencies would be reduced to the level of small ones, the Association and not the electors would return the Member. The claim of any Association, however respectable, to exercise such a power, would, in my judgement, be at variance with those principles of political reform and electoral freedom which have always been the watchword of the Liberal Party...For a body of gentlemen to form themselves into an association in order to introduce a candidate of their choice and to use all lawful influence to secure his return, is a perfectly fair and legitimate object; but it is quite another thing for them to call upon a candidate to bind himself beforehand to submit to a possible ostracism and by so narrowing a field of choice to deprive a whole constituency or a whole political party of the opportunity of exercising the undoubted right to return the man they would most prefer."

(The Times, 6th October 1879)

The electoral success of the Caucus was startling, and it spread over the rest of the country. It carried with it an inherent challenge to the official leadership of the Liberal Party. Gladstone, however, saw the possibilities of this system and gave it his most ardent support. In doing so, he avoided the open clash of authority which would otherwise have arisen; he retained the personal loyalty of the Caucus members.

Chamberlain, as organiser of the Caucus, and therefore a potential rival to the Liberal Party leadership, was thus outstripped by Gladstone. When in the Home Rule crisis, Chamberlain declared against Gladstone, he failed to carry the Caucus with him, and he left the Liberal Party. Gladstone removed the Caucus from Birmingham and joined it to the Whip's office, under whose absolute control it fell. The democratic mechanism, known as the Liberal Federation, was allowed to continue, and it had the effect of strengthening the central office control of the constituency organisations by giving it a semblance of democratic basis. There is nothing harder to discern than a dictatorship which disguises itself as a democracy, but it is in such a guise that the Liberal Party lost its soul, and finally ceased to have any influence. But its form of organisation had a decisive influence on the development of the party system as we know it today.

In the case of the Conservative Party, the same ends were attained, but the process was different. The party was never so deeply committed to the democratic idea, and Disraeli, though the author of the Reform Act, rejected the idea of a democratic party. The democratic challenge came after his death through the agency of Lord Randolph Churchill and his demand for Tory democracy. He attempted, and to some extent succeeded, in creating a Conservative Party organisation based upon the Liberal Party Caucus plan. His efforts, however, in fighting the Conservative Central Office and the Parliamentary leadership failed, and the organisation he had created was transferred to the management of the Central Office, which thereby acquired the boon of a democratic façade to the party organisation. But the basic principle of the party system which Disraeli had laid down made such a façade really unnecessary.

Disraeli's influence on the theory of our modern party system is outstanding, and it dominates all conceptions of political democracy, especially in the new parties associated with the working class movement after the Chartist Parliamentary traditions had died out. Disraeli's pronouncement in favour of the "Leadership principle" based on militarised parties is one of the most far-reaching influences on the progress of 20th century civilisation in England and the Continent.

The party organisation crisis following the Reform Act of 1867 had reached a culminating point ten years later. Disraeli, or rather Lord Beaconsfield , as he had become, had also reached the culminating point of his career with the Congress of Berlin. He returned in triumph with his "Peace with Honour", a national god. A deputation of the newly formed Conservative Associations for England and Wales met him on August 6th, 1878, and in answer to their congratulations on his triumph, he addressed them as follows:-

> "There is, I think, a very great error prevalent that opinion when organised loses something of its genuineness and force. I believe that is a great and most pernicious fallacy. I believe opinion, when organised, loses nothing of its genuineness and sincerity. On the contrary, when shaped by the result of considerable thought and some experience, there is a greater chance of opinion actuating and influencing mankind. It cannot be supposed for a moment that when opinion is organised it loses any of its force, because that idea would contradict the experience of mankind in all ages.
>
> All men have agreed that in the conduct of public affairs, there is nothing more precious than discipline, and it is a great mistake to think that discipline is incompatible with the deepest convictions and even the most passionate sentiments. Whether we look into military affairs in ancient or modern times, we see many illustrations of that principle. I suppose that there never was a body of men animated by a higher degree of patriotism, or who extended their influence through a longer period, than the Roman Legion; and the Roman Legion was a model of discipline. So again, when the Macedonians contemplated conquering the world they formed their phalanx; and though they were animated by so great an idea, still no one denied that it was the discipline of the Macedonian phalanx which contributed to the conquest of Asia.

And in our times and history, there are numerous illustrations. I suppose there never was a more disciplined body of men in warfare than Cromwell's troopers, and they were influenced by the highest degree of religious feeling; and in our own immediate past, the Peninsular heroes, whose achievements are now recognised as almost unparalleled, were men who were animated to the last thought - devotion to their leader (loud cheers) and yet it is a well known fact that at the end of several years over which the Peninsular campaign extended, there never was a period in which the discipline was so severe as in the last year, and in which the regulations were welcomed with more cheerfulness by the soldiers who served under that great man who said that as a consequence of their discipline, he could do anything with his army and go anywhere. I make these remarks because there is a very prevalent idea, and for it there is some foundation, that when men are acting in a corporate capacity they sometimes forget principles which assembled them together originally and their acting together degenerates into a mere routine.

I do not deny that there is some foundation for that opinion, but it is an evil which, if we were subjected to it, can be counteracted by the efforts of those I see before me - the officers of the great constitutional army which was formed throughout the country and disciplined until it obtained the triumphant results which the recent general election established. (Loud Cheers). No doubt there was a time when there were Pitt clubs formed; because pains were not taken to construct them in great principles which would keep them together, they became obsolete and disappeared. I am convinced that it is impossible that we rate too highly in public life the magical effect of discipline."

(The Times, 7th August 1878)

The significance of these words of the Conservative Party leader was not lost on contemporary public opinion. The leading article of "The Times" gives us an insight into the foreboding effect these words produced. "The Times", in discussing this speech of Lord Beaconsfield in the issue in which it was reported, included the following in its remarks:-

> "There is not, it will be evident, much to choose between Liberal Caucuses and Conservative Associations. There seems in fact to be a kind of growing competition in severity between their discipline. The Birmingham tactics were provoked, if not suggested, by the success of the strict organisation which has for some time past, been characteristic of the Conservative Party and it is now, in turn, to be outdone by the conservatives themselves. The little finger of Lord Beaconsfield, even in his hour of success, is to be heavier than Mr Gladstone's whole hand.
>
> We are to choose between Liberal Caucuses and Conservative phalanxes, but in neither party are we to remain our own masters. If Mr Gladstone is to be a dictator, Lord Beaconsfield is to be transformed into an emperor. With his legions, his phalanxes, his ironsides and his troopers, that can go anywhere and do anything, he is to proceed from victory to victory, and if his followers will only thus believe in the "magical" effects of discipline they may never expect to lose their hold over the Government of England. Such is the political prospect before us at the close of a great political crisis...
>
> We are henceforth to be rigidly divided into two camps, within each of which the discipline is to be unbending. Private idiosyncrasies, local foibles all that gives colour and diversity to discussion, is to be suppressed lest it should involve hesitation in action. Candidates are no longer to stand on their own merits or to depend on their personal influence over the component members of the constituency. They are to be imposed once and for all by an external authority and are then to be accepted

as inevitable. We see in all this a great deal of the order which Lord Beaconsfield extols as characteristics of English life, but very little of the liberty …It is only to be hoped that English instinct will, after all, be a little too strong for the transformation of political into military organisation to be rendered complete. When one party would hoodwink us and the other party would dragoon us into uniformity, there is now more need than ever for English independence to assert itself in occasional "eccentricity. "

(The Times, 8th August 1878)

Already at the time these words were being penned, there was a stirring in the political field, which was eventually to result in the growth and successful establishment of the Labour and Socialist organisation, which was to replace the Liberal Party as the second party in the nation.

Francis Holland, in his continuation of May's "Constitutional History of England", has given us a summary of what "democracy" means in our party organisation, especially in relation to the Labour Party, when he writes:-

"Party discipline has, in the case of the Labour Party been carried to the point previously unknown in English political life. The object aimed at by the Caucus associations of the two great parties, namely, the subordination of the private judgement of the individual member to the collective decision of the party, has been expressly formulated and enshrined in the constitution of the Labour Party."

(Vol. 3, p. 139)

No party is louder than the Labour Party in its democratic protestations, yet in the organisation of the party in its annual conference, there is little which could be described as conforming to democratic principle. On the contrary, every conceivable device has been introduced to prevent the party membership from having an effective voice in party activity or decisions.

For this party, which in national affairs professes on democratic grounds to allow one vote to one person, regardless of any other consideration, permits within its own party constitution a handful of non-political delegates to outvote the thousand delegates representing the whole political section of the party. It is indeed remarkable what a wide interpretation can be given to the meaning of democracy where the parties themselves are concerned. Not one of them has ever applied the principle of majority rule on the basis of one member one vote.

The implication of the militarised organisation of the British political party system has been fully recognised. J. L. Garvin, for many years the famous editor of the "Observer" in his biography of Joseph Chamberlain, defends his hero from contemporary attacks but, in a few sentences, betrays the significance of his party's political activity. When he described the success of the Caucus in Birmingham, he wrote:-

> "A few weeks after the local elections, the full power of the Birmingham system appeared at the General Election of 1874. In the midst of Conservative triumphs elsewhere, that party did not care to face a contest in this almost Fascist citadel of Radicalism - as we might say today without paradox or exaggeration."

(Life of Joseph Chamberlain, Vol. 1, p. 255)

How general this Fascist principle has become to the whole of our party system, Garvin himself bears witness. A few pages on, when he summarises Chamberlain's achievements as a machine politician Garvin writes:-

> "We have seen that the Liberal Caucus, at every stage, owed its strongest traits in a very English way to a spirit of resistance. It arose when new forms of combination were a general social tendency. It was as natural as Trade Unionism. All organisation - though the purpose be the highest, as in religion -brings its penalties. 'When spirit seeks to master flesh gross flesh invades it'. The Birmingham system as nationally and locally applied, had its episodes of intrigue and vendetta. Sometimes, perhaps often, wire-pulling did

manufacture appearance of popular feeling not in fact corresponding to the true balance of public opinion. Adopted by every party in Great Britain and Ireland this system was more and more used by all of them to deter and crush personal independence."

(Ibid. p. 264)

The crushing of personal independence is the outstanding and fearful feature of the totalitarian party dictatorships.

No less significant by their implication are the words of the biographer of the creator of the Conservative party machine, which above all things stood and still claims to stand for the preservation of the constitution. George Earle Buckle, in the fifth volume of the "Life of Benjamin Disraeli," thus summarises the part Disraeli played in the creation of the modern English party system: -

"Disraeli was responsible for starting the first great party machine, and he reaped the harvest in the victory of 1874. But, though experience here and elsewhere seems to prove that party organisations are essential to democratic government, Disraeli's judicious admirers are hardly likely to claim much credit for him on the score of this feat. As might have been expected, the Liberals bettered the Conservatives' example by perfecting the Birmingham Caucus, and extending its operations to the whole country; and the machine became so highly organised on both sides as to make increasingly difficult the entry into the House of Commons, and the continuance there, of those independent politicians to secure whose adhesions it was necessary for Government to look beyond party...Hence there has come a serious decline of parliamentary control over Ministers; and a great accession of power to the statesman or the party committee who may happen to have commanded at the preceding election the support of the majority of the constituencies."

(Page 186)

There is only one possible conclusion to be derived from the discipline and leader principle of our modern party system as it has been developed by Disraeli and organised by Chamberlain. The party system in England is fundamentally totalitarian in principle and anti-democratic in practice.

This modern militarised party system has created a political monopoly by which the wide knowledge and experience of the British people has been excluded from responsible public activity. Our national administration is now in the hands of a small class of professional Party politicians who, by their control of Parliament, have established their own rules under which they have relieved themselves of all effective public responsibility. A great nation of 50 million people with a responsibility covering at one time hundreds of millions, derives its leadership and national administration from a small capricious circle of less than 400 professional politicians in a Party controlled Parliament. These high positions are filled not by election but by appointment made not by methods known to ensure the supremacy of national considerations but solely on Party grounds, frequently due to pressure groups and wire pulling behind the scenes, of which the nation knows nothing. The qualifications for these high and significant positions are not apparent. We are not expected to assume there are any. The political qualifications which are to be presumed are all sufficient. Thus we find all the highest and most significant positions of the greatest influence to our national destiny filled on grounds which can only be described as political nepotism on the largest scale.

It is true in theory that there is a right to establish a new party and, if sufficient electoral support is forthcoming to obtain a majority in the House of Commons, to appoint the Cabinet from its own members. In actual practice, however, the principle of Party government rejects multiplicity of parties, and every influence is exerted to hinder the formation of a new Party. The Party system in Britain is basically a two party system. In consequence, every form of interest and opinion has to find a place in one or other of the two Parties so that each Party is a cloak covering a multiplicity of opinions and interests, each of which is struggling for the control of the party machine on issues which seldom appear in public The victory of one group over another may completely alter the character, nature, ideology and direction of the Party and yet nothing may appear as to the fundamental changes that have taken place.

It is true that Parties have programmes and profess to have principles that they combine with election pledges, but no political party is or can be bound by its own commitments or declarations, however solemn the undertaking. The Party system, therefore, amounts to no more than giving the people a choice of Party labels with no real knowledge or assurance as to what any label stands for. Elections are, in fact, blind and are merely a process by which the power of the people is unconditionally surrendered into the control of politicians who exercise immense powers of the state under no legal or constitutional restraint. The minority party in the House of Commons has no means of restraining the majority except by the prospective threat at the time of the next election, when it hopes to replace the existing government. Is it likely that the Opposition will restrain or restrict the powers of Government which it hopes soon to enjoy?

By making national policy dependent upon Party rivalry, national authority rests on nothing firmer than Party expediency, unstable and fickle. The rivalry between the Party organisations is activated by passion and emotion, fed by ignorance and prejudice, and is ever a focus of conflict and disruption. Under the rule of politics, basic human rights are subject to the operation of forces governed by uninhibited self interests regardless of the rights of the individual and the needs of the community; only modified by political expediency, and gilded over with specious idealism in which injustice is exploited for political ends. R.T. McKenzie, in his textbook "British Political Parties," has pointed out:-

> "The study of the psychology of political processes has revealed the importance of the extra-rational and irrational elements in social behaviour. The parallel development of the arts of political propaganda has enabled political leaders to exploit the irrational elements in human behaviour and to manufacture what is often a purely synthetic 'general will' so much so that some people are prepared to argue ...that the will of the people is the product and not the motive power of the political process."

(page580)

Such a system creates by the competition for power between the parties and within the party organisations themselves, a constant turmoil and turbulence in national affairs and makes impossible that stability and sense of common unity upon which alone national and even civilised progress can be achieved.

Under the Party system, the vision of a nation living in time is made impossible by the overpowering urge of winning or retaining power at the next election. The past means little, and the generations to come have no vote; only the mass electorate now in existence counts and its ignorance and passions are exploited as the condition of exercising power. The consequence is that the Party system not only has little conception of the meaning of statesmanship but is deeply jealous of its manifestation, whether it is in its own ranks or outside them. The Party system has to specialise in one thing , and one thing only - tactics, political tactics. In military affairs tactics are an essential element in the development of strategy, but where there is no statesmanship, there is no national strategy, and this reduces political tactics to a most sordid level of chaotic contradictions in which there can be no consistent national policy either at home or abroad. In such conditions, any quality of statesmanship which may still be found in public life atrophies and disappears. The statesman is helpless. He can rise to power only by subjecting his integrity, his knowledge, his experience and his sense of patriotism to the demands of Party discipline. If his character can survive years of such conditioning and he finds himself in high office, he no longer has that freedom from Party considerations which would enable him always to look to the public good. The pursuit of any long-term policy becomes impossible. Whatever he does, it must be related to Party exigencies and the next election.

In his work "The Second World War," Sir Winston Churchill gave a judgement on our political system at a period of great national crisis, which must ring true in every heart however much one may disagree with any issue involved. He wrote:-

> "We must regard as deeply blameworthy before history
> the conduct, not only of the British National and mainly
> Conservative party Government, but of the Labour-
> Socialist and Liberal Parties both in and out of office
> during this fatal period. Delight in smooth sounding
> platitudes, refusal to face unpleasant facts, desire for
> popularity and electoral success irrespective of the
> vital interests of the State, genuine love of peace and

pathetic belief that love can be its sole foundation, obvious lack of intellectual vigour in both leaders of the British Coalition Government... the whole supported by overwhelming majorities in the both Houses of Parliament; all these constituted a picture of British fatuity and fickleness which, though devoid of guile, was not devoid of guilt, and though free from wickedness or evil design, played a definite part in the unleashing upon the world the horrors and miseries which, even so far as they have unfolded, are already beyond comparison in human experience."

(The Gathering Storm, Vol. 1, p.69)

The party system neither claims nor pretends to be bound by any constitutional or even democratic considerations. Lord Hewart, in "The New Despotism", cites only cases of despotic legislation passed by the so-called constitutional parties. The Labour Party, on the whole, has been very timid in departing from so called "constitutional" practice which the other parties had established, but it gave clear and definite warning that it meant to exploit to the full every constitutional precedent provided by their opponents.

We have, for example, the warning given by J.H. Clynes, one of the most conservative of the Labour leaders. This is what he said with regard to the Emergency Powers Act of 1931:-

"We regard the Act as utterly un-British and unconstitutional. If in such a time as this, in the days of peace, it is right and constitutional for a government to settle things swiftly by Orders in Council, without amendment and question will it not be equally right on some later day, when there is a majority Labour Government, to get a bill through to its second reading and then decree through Orders in Council the nationalisation of the land of England? We might in some future years get our proposals through the House of Commons with greater speed than many Conservatives now imagine."

(Manchester Guardian, 16th Sept. 1931)

The parties, both the so-called constitutional and progressive, have no objection whatsoever to their members holding and expressing totalitarian views provided they remain loyal to the party system itself. Less than a year before the outbreak of the second world war, Sir Winston Churchill expressed the hope that a Hitler would arise in England. (The Times, 7th November 1938) Sir Oswald Mosely was condemned not because he was a Fascist in his views but because he opposed the party system itself. He had been preaching an authoritarian policy for years in the Labour Party. Take, for example, his speech on 2nd August 1926:-

> "One of the effective instruments for carrying out a drastic socialist policy under the Labour Government is the present Emergency Powers Act. He hoped, therefore, that the Socialists would not be unduly critical of it. Under this act, a Labour Government would nationalise land, mines, banking and other essential services in the event of an economic breakdown and could even seize all social property without payment or compensation.
>
> In the event of obstruction by the possessors a Labour Government could arrest or imprison them in the same way the present Government had done with the strikers during the past three months. He didn't believe that piecemeal Socialism would be of any use to this country and the Socialists must be prepared in the spirit of Cromwell's Ironsides, to wage their cause strenuously against the fiercest opposition that would be offered by the possessing classes."
>
> (Manchester Guardian)

For holding such views, Sir Oswald was not excluded from his party. He was selected later with general approval to the National Executive of the Labour Party and was made an important member of the Labour Government in 1929, before he himself went into opposition to the party system.

Mr C. R. (later Earl) Atlee, before he became Prime Minister, wrote in 1933 in "Problems of a Socialist Government":-

> "The important thing is not to do things with the most scrupulous regard to the theories of democracy or exact constitutional propriety, but to get on with the job…"

When he came to deal with his ideas on local Government, Earl Atlee went on to write:-

> "I conceive the District Commissioner as something more than a public servant. He is the local energiser and interpreter on the will of the government. He is not impartial. He is a Socialist and therefore in touch with the Socialists in the region who are his colleagues in his campaign. It may be said that this is rather like the Russian plan of Commissars and Communist Party members. I am not afraid of the comparison. We have to take the strong points of the Russian system and apply them to this country."

Sir Stafford Cripps, KC., at one time an influential force in the Labour Party and a leading English lawyer, had even more emphatic totalitarian ideas than Sir Oswald Mosely. Speaking at the Fabian Summer School in 1932, he declared:-

> "Just as the spirit of the Communist Party organisation in Russia has made possible by the operation of the Five year Plan, so the transition to Socialism will only be possible in this country by a party inspired with a sense of devotion and solidarity which alone can be the motive power for the transition…That should be the great lesson for us of the Russian experiment. Once the Party is in power, it will have to be ruthless as regards individuals."

(Where stands Socialism today)

This can now be established in constitutional terms. In the same speech, Sir Stafford Cripps declared:-

"For one thing, we may, I think be grateful to the National Government. They have made full use of the principle of the flexibility of our constitution. With a flexible constitution unwritten and capable of immediate and fundamental alteration at a moment's notice much can be done, much indeed has been done in the last year. It is upon these precedents - themselves now part of the constitution-that the Labour Party will have to act...In theory Parliament can hand over any or all its powers to any Minister or outside body it chooses for as long as it wishes. Such powers must, of course always remain under the ultimate control of the Government, that is of the Cabinet. All that is necessary is for Parliament to decide the ambit of the powers so handed over and the manner of their exercise...It is possible now for an individual to challenge in the Courts, the use of any particular power so exercised by a Minister as being outside the sphere as determined by Parliament. This inconvenience must be removed , as it can be in the legislation granting the powers. The question of validity of Orders made under Acts of Parliament giving powers to legislate by Order in Council should be reserved for decision by Parliament, and should be incapable of being raised after a short time, if at all."

(Where stands Socialism today)

Never at any time have such views been condemned as subversive or even declared unconstitutional. We have here expressed the ultimate power claimed by the Party system by its control of the membership of the House of Commons.

THE CORRUPTION OF PARLIAMENT

The corruption of Parliament was defined by Burke in "Present Discontents" when he wrote:-

> "For my part, I shall be compelled to include the principle of Parliament to be totally corrupted and its end entirely defeated when I see two symptoms; first a rule of indiscriminate support to all Ministers; because this destroys the very end of Parliament as a control and is a general sanction to misgovernment; and secondly, the setting up of any claims adverse to the right of free election, for this tends to subvert the legal authority by which the House of Commons sits."

> (The Works of Edmund Burke, World Classics, LXXI, Vol.2, p.52)

It is this corruption of Parliament which the party System has established as its principle of government and extended it into every corner of the constitution.

Parliament is the supreme organ of English national authority for it is in Parliament that the whole nation is brought into a single court.

Sir Thomas Smith, Secretary of State to Queen Elizabeth I, pointed out in his "De Republica Anglorum":-

> "Every Englishman is intended to be there present in person or by procuration and attornies of what pre-eminent state, dignity or quality, soever he be, from the Prince (be he King or Queen) to the lowest person in England. And the consent of Parliament is taken to be every man's consent."

> (Page 49)

This was confirmed by Parliament in the Act of Recognition of James I, where it is enacted that:-

> "In the High Court of Parliament where the whole body of the realm and every particular member thereof either in person or by representation (upon their own free election) are by the laws of this realm deemed to be personally present."

> (The Statutes at Large, Vol. 2, I Jac. C. IS. II,1603, p. 336)

Parliament is thus the supreme legal tribunal of the English nation. As Coke put it in the reign of Elizabeth I:-

> "Parliament is the highest and most honourable and absolute Court of Justice in England consisting of the King, the Lords of Parliament and the Commons.

> (1st Inst. Sec .110a)

Like all legal tribunals, Parliament is subject to the law from which it derives its supremacy and by which its jurisdiction is defined. Parliament is therefore, subject to certain fundamental laws which Parliament cannot defy without ceasing to be a legally constituted supreme authority. Among such fundamental laws, Parliament cannot make itself perpetual, nor can Parliament abdicate its authority into other hands nor delegate its supremacy. There are, however, three fundamental laws upon which the authority of Parliament must rest and which are recognised in form.

The first fundamental law of Parliament is Parliament exists only by the co-ordination of its three institutions, each supreme in one or other aspect of national authority but each of which is subject to the law of the land which not one can change without the consent in written form of the other two.

The first institution of Parliament is the King representing the eminent domain of the nation, acting as the supreme governor and sworn at his coronation service to rule under God and the Law and from whom all legal authority including that of Parliament is derived. As under the doctrine that the King can do no wrong, he is able to act only with the advice and consent of his ministers appointed by him for their skill and capacity but subject to the continuous confidence of the House of Commons. Every minister or anyone else appointed by the Crown is responsible personally and criminally for all acts of authority or for advice tendered, on impeachment by the House of Commons for high crimes and misdemeanours.

The second institution of Parliament is the House of Lords, a senate originally appointed by the Crown but independent of the Crown being the supreme court of English law acting with the advice of the whole bench of English Judges and as the court of first instance on all impeachments by the House of Commons.

The third institution of Parliament is the elected House of commons acting as the Grand Inquest of the nation as the control on government and judicial authority and active in the redress of grievances armed with the supreme or rather sole power of taxation.

The second fundamental law of Parliament is that each of the three institutions of Parliament is totally independent from either of the other two or from outside influence and control for as Blackstone put it in his "Commentaries on the Laws of England":-

> "For if ever it should happen that the independence of any one of the three should be lost, or that it should become subservient to the views of either of the other two, there would soon be an end of our constitution."

(introduction, Sec. 2, p.51)

The third fundamental law of Parliament is that all elections to the House of Commons must be free for it is through the House of Commons that the people express their consent to legislation and by which all infringements of law by rulers or powerful subjects can be restrained and corrected.

As Chief Justice Holt declared in his minority judgement in the case of the Aylesbury men in 1704:-

> "By the Common Law of England, every commoner hath a right not to be subjected to laws made without his consent, and because it cannot be given by every individual man in person by reason of number and

confusion, therefore, that power is lodged in the representatives elected by them for that purpose."

Parliament thus legally constituted, is the assurance that the authority of Parliament is never arbitrary, despotic, capricious nor governed by passion and emotion but is actuated by reason which alone can bring three independent and diverse institutions to a common agreement and ensures above all that all law is derived solely from the consent of the people.

It is therefore fundamental to the whole institution and authority of Parliament that only when its three co-ordinate institutions reach independently of each other a common agreement in written form that the absolute supremacy of Parliament exists in the form as Coke expressed it:-

> "...of the power and jurisdiction of the Parliament for the making of laws in proceeding by Bill, it is so transcendent and absolute as it cannot be confined for either causes or persons within any bounds."

(4th Inst. Page 36.)

The main spring of Parliament has ever been English Law derived from the consent of her people by which every corruption of power by rulers and subjects has been defeated through the centuries of English history.

Today we are faced with the corruption of Parliament itself by the violation of the freedom of election to the House of Commons.

The freedom of election goes beyond the mere mechanics of the election process but must cover the freedom of nomination and the freedom of the person elected from the influence of fear of punishment or the favour of patronage.

Blackstone, in his "Commentaries on the Laws of England", points out:-

> "As it is essential to the very being of Parliament that elections should be absolutely free, therefore all undue influence upon the electors are illegal and strongly prohibited. For Mr. Locke ranks it among those branches

of trust in the executive magistrate, which according to his notions, amount to a dissolution of the government, if he employs the force, treasure and offices of the society to corrupt the representative or openly to pre-engage the electors, and prescribe what manner of persons shall be chosen. For thus to regulate candidates and electors and new-model the ways of election, what is it 'he says' but to cut up the government by the roots and poison the very fountain of public security."

(Book 1, Ch. 2, p. 173)

By undermining the freedom of election to the House of Commons, the modern Party system has not only destroyed the independence of the House of Commons but the independence and integrity of the other two institutions of Parliament and thus destroyed the whole legal mechanism of Parliamentary supremacy, which it has now usurped.

The principle of free elections has been the condition of a legal House of Commons ever since its institution. The first Statute of Westminster of 1275 in the reign of Edward I enacted, and the words still stand in our statute book:-

"...and because elections ought to be free, the King commandeth upon great forfeitur that no man by force of arms, nor by malice or menacing shall disturb any to make free elections.

(The Statutes Revised, 2nd edition. Statute of Westminster 1, 1275, p. 10)

The first serious concerted attempt to do this was made by Richard II. In the Articles of Accusation made against him by the Estates of Parliament and which led to his virtual deposition in the revolution of 1399, the first one read:-

"Although by the statute and custom of this realm in the calling together of every Parliament, his people in the several countries of the kingdom ought to be free in choosing and deputing two knights to be present in such Parliament, for each respective country, and to declare their grievances and to prosecute such remedies thereupon as to them shall be expedient; yet the aforesaid King, that in his Parliament he might be more freely to accomplish the effects of his headstrong will, did very often direct his commands to his sheriff's that they should cause to come to his Parliament as knights of the shire certain persons by the said King named; which knights being his favourites, he might lead, as often as he had done, sometimes by various menaces and terrors, and sometimes by gifts, to consent to those things as were prejudicial to the kingdom and exceedingly burdensome to the people.."

(State Trials, Vol.1 Col. 145)

In the Revolution of 1688, resulting in the abdication of James II, similar accusations were made against him by William of Orange in his declaration before landing in England and which included the following passage:-

"Though according to the constitution of the English government, and immemorial customs, all elections of Parliament men ought to be made with an entire liberty without any sort of force or requiring of the electors to choose such persons as shall be named to them, and the persons thus freely elected ought to give their opinions freely upon all matters that are brought before them having the good of the nation ever before their eyes, and following in all things the dictates of their conscience, yet now the people of England cannot expect a remedy from a Free Parliament, legally called and chosen. But they may, perhaps see one called, in which all elections will be carried by force, and which will be composed of such persons, of whom these evil councillors hold themselves assured, in which all things will be carried on according to their directions and interest, without regard to the goodness and happiness of the nation."

(From the Declaration of his Highness William Henry, Prince of Orange, for the reasons inducing him to

appear in arms in the Kingdom of England. Hague. 10th
October 1688)

As a protection against any repetition of this abuse the great
constitutional enactment known as The Bill of Rights with provisions
specifically dealing with the freedom of elections was enacted by
Parliament. One clause reads:-

> "The election of members of Parliament ought to
> be free."

As freedom of election must also cover the freedom of elected
representatives, a further clause in the Bill of Rights lays it down that:-

> "...the freedom of speech and debates or proceedings in
> Parliament ought not to be impeached or questioned in
> any court or place out of Parliament."

In 1938 the House of Commons set up a select committee charged
with the task of enquiring:-

> "Into the applicability of the Official Secrets Act to
> members of this House in the discharge of their
> Parliamentary duties, having regard for the undoubted
> privileges of this House as confirmed in the Bill
> of Rights."

The Committee in its report (101, 5th April 1939), drew attention to the
fact that the term "Proceedings in Parliament" had never been construed
by the Courts, but it accepted the view that it would be unreasonable to
conclude that no act is within the scope of a member's duties in the course
of Parliamentary business unless it is done in the House or a committee
thereof and while the House or committee is sitting. Clause 13 of the
Report of the Committee stated:-

> "Sir Gilbert Campion pointed out that, by the law of
> Parliament, as declared in the Bill of Rights, not only
> may debates and proceedings in Parliament not be
> questioned elsewhere, but freedom of speech may not
> be 'impeached' in any court or place out of Parliament,

and further was of opinion that when the Bill of Rights was passed 'to impeach' still retained its original signification of impeding, preventing or hindering...."

Clause 23 of the same Report declared that:-

"your Committee would emphasise a point mentioned in the Report which they made to the House in the last session of Parliament, namely, that the privilege of freedom of speech enjoyed by members of Parliament is in truth the privilege of their constituents. It is secured to members not for their personal benefit but to enable them to discharge the functions of their office without fear of prosecution civil or criminal. The Commons in their famous protestation of 1621 declared the privileges of Parliament to be the birthright and inheritance of the subject. There are, no doubt, dangers even in the limited immunity from prosecution under the Official Secrets Acts secured to members by parliamentary privilege. But they are dangers which must be run if members are to continue to exercise their traditional right and duty of criticising the executive. 'Parliaments without parliamentary liberties', said Pym, 'are but a fair and plausible way into bondage', and it remains as true today as it was in 1610 that 'freedom of debate once foreclosed, the essence of the liberty of Parliament is withal dissolved'."

One point calls for particular attention. Discussion on the clause of the Bill of Rights is based on the assumption that it is concerned only with protection from legal action in the courts. But the wording of the clause and as repeated by Sir Gilbert Campion states most specifically 'court or place out of Parliament'.

The corruption of Parliament has its source in the political monopoly which the party system has established in the nomination of candidates for election to the House of Commons.

Professor Berriedale Keith, in the seventh edition of Ridge's "Constitutional Law of England", points out:-

"A member is carefully selected with regard to the Party tenets and leader; and on this rests his chance of office or honour or other advancement for himself or friends, and his power of influencing the Ministry to take up legislation in which he is interested and give if introduced as a private member's Bill; if he deserts the party on an important issue, his superiors will object; a dissolution may result, and he will probably lose his seat, and in any case will have to fight without aid in funds or central approval."

(Page 15)

The late Rt. Hon. L. S. Amery, in "Thoughts on the Constitution," points out that:-

"At a general election, the voter is not in a position to choose either the kind of representative or the kind of government he would like if he had a free choice. There is a Government which he can confirm or else reject in favour of the alternative team. The candidates before him - the only candidates worth taking seriously - are either supporters of the team in office or its rivals for office. It is within these narrow limits that his actual power is exercised."

(Page 16)

Professor Ramsey Muir in "How Britain is Governed", points out that the power of the voter:-

"...is in fact limited to indicating a preference between two or three candidates whom (as a rule) he has had no voice in selecting. They may all be totally unknown to him; they may all seem to him objectionable, and unfit for the performance of important public functions; but he must either make a choice between them, or abdicate his civic right."

(page 5)

The immediate effect of the party monopoly of nominations of candidates (strengthened by the deposit of £150 which is lost if insufficient votes are recorded) is that candidates are bound to the party and have therefore no independence.

By this monopoly of party candidates to the House of Commons, the party system is able to establish a complete control over the membership of the House of Commons.

Professor Ramsey Muir in "How Britain is Governed", points out that:-

> "Party organisations and party discipline have been so much elaborated during the last two generations, that the Members of Parliament who have been elected as representatives of a party, hesitate long before showing any independence of their leaders or, at any rate, before carrying their independence to the point of open revolt, because they know they will thus endanger their seats; in a system of elections based upon single member constituencies, as ours is, the ablest man has little or no chance of election if a rival candidate is put up against him by his own party."

(Page 25)

In Professor Berriedale Keith's "The British Cabinet System, 1830-1938", it is stated that:-

> "Yet another consideration weighs heavily with the recalcitrant member. If he falls from grace the whips will report his activities to the constituencies association, and he will be refused their imprimatur if he seeks re-election. Without it very few members can hope for a new term of membership and very few men are eager to fight an election at their own cost and with scant prospect of success.

(Page 267)

It cannot be denied that members of Parliament are called before the central committees of their party organisations to explain their votes and activities in Parliament before they are excluded from a Parliamentary career unless they mend their ways. All this can only mean that a member of Parliament is impeached outside Parliament for his proceedings in Parliament. This is nothing less than an outrage against our Parliamentary institutions, which, though several attempted it, not one King of England throughout our long history succeeded in perpetrating.

When members of Parliament put themselves under the discipline of a party machine which controls their actions and utterances and which dictates how they are to vote in Parliament, they are betraying an essential privilege of Parliament. What is more, they are betraying a privilege which is not theirs to sacrifice, for it is the birthright of those whom they purport to represent. It is the docile betrayal of this essential condition of English Liberty, which accounts for the dangerous decay of our Parliamentary institutions and for the ever-growing contempt of those who are members of it. Under the whip of the party leaders, the House of Commons is now precisely what Burke insisted that it should not be. In his speech to the electors of Bristol on November 3rd, 1773, Burke declared:-

> "To deliver an opinion is the right of all men; that of a constituent is a weighty and respectable opinion, which a representative ought always to rejoice to hear and which he ought always most seriously to consider, but authoritative instructions, mandates issued which the member is bound blindly and implicitly to obey, to vote and to argue for, though contrary to the clearest conviction of his judgement and conscience -these are utterly unknown to the laws of the land and which arise from a fundamental mistake of the whole order and tenor of our constitution.
>
> Parliament is not a congress of ambassadors from different and hostile interests, which interest each man must maintain as an agent and advocate against other agents and other advocates; but Parliament is a deliberative assembly of one nation with one interest, that of the whole, where not local purpose or local prejudices, ought to guide, but the general good

resulting from the general reason of the whole. You choose a member indeed, but when you have chosen him, he is not a member of Bristol, but he is a member of Parliament."

(The works of Edmund Burke, World Classics, LXXXI, p. 165)

Today the House of Commons membership acts on the mandate of the Party system which they are bound implicitly to obey and which has divided them into hostile groups thus destroying the House of Commons as the representative organ of the united nation.

By its control of the membership of the House of Commons, the Party system has effectively destroyed the central principle of the English Parliamentary Constitution by which there lies a responsibility to Parliament both criminal and political by all who exercise any authority whatsoever.

Ministerial responsibility to Parliament is fundamental and was clearly set out in 1627 in the early years of the reign of Charles I by the House of Commons in their humble remonstrance to the King which declared:-

"Now concerning your majesty's servants and namely the Duke of Buckingham, we humbly beseech your majesty to be informed by us, your faithful Commons, who can have no private end but your Majesty's service and the good of our country; that it hath been the ancient constant and undoubted right and usage of Parliament, to question and complain of all persons of what degree whatsoever, found grievous to the Commonwealth, in abusing the power and trust committed to them by their sovereign, a course approved not only by the example of your father's days of famous memory, but by frequent precedents in the best and most glorious reigns of your noble progenitors, appearing both in records and histories, without which liberty in Parliament, no private man, no servant to a King, perhaps no councillor without exposing himself to the hazard of great enmity and prejudice, can be a means to call great officers in question for their misdemeanours, but the commonwealth might languish under their pressure without redress."

(Historical Collections, Rushworth, Vol.1, p.249)

This responsibility is enforced by the House of Commons by impeachment for high crimes and misdemeanours and tried by the House of Lords as the supreme court of English Law.

Speaking in Westminster Hall on 5th February 1788. Edmund Burke declared:-

"If the constitution be deprived, I do not mean in form, but virtually of this resource, it is virtually deprived of everything else that is valuable in it. For this process is the cement which binds the whole together; this is the individuating principle that makes England what England is. In this high court of Parliament it is that no subjects, in no part of the empire can fail of the competent and proportionable justice; here it is that we provide for that which is the substantial excellence of our constitution; I mean the great circulation of responsibility, by which no man, in no circumstances, can escape that account which he owes to the laws of this country.

It is by this process that magistracy, which tries and controls all other things, is itself tried and controlled. Other constitutions are satisfied with making good subjects; this is the security for good governors. It is by this tribunal that statesmen, who abuse their power, are accused by statesmen, and tried by statesmen, not upon the niceties of a narrow jurisprudence but upon enlarged and solid principles of state morality. It is here that these who by the abuse of power have violated the spirit of law, can never hope for protection from any of its forms; it is here that those who have refused to confine themselves to its perfection, can never hope to escape through any of its defects."

(The Works of Edmund Burke, Bohn. British Classics, 18577, Vol. VII, p. 10)

There was a time when the King himself was responsible to Parliament for the lawful exercise of his prerogative. We have the case of Richard II, accused by the estates of Parliament and deposed for claiming to exercise an authority not bound by law. The settlement of the revolution of 1399 was based on the promise of Henry IV that he would rule with the advice and consent of his council. From this, the doctrine was established that the King can do no wrong. This means that though all national authority is exercised in his name, the King, in his personal capacity, can execute no office or perform no act of government without the advice and consent of his Ministers. He may not even arrest a burglar that he may discover in his palace. As Lord Erskine declared in the House of Lords on 13th April, 1807:-

"The King can perform no act of government himself and no man ought to be received within the walls of this House to declare that any act of the government has proceeded from the private will and determination or conscience of the King. The King as chief magistrate can have no conscience, which is not the trust of responsible subjects. When he delivers the seals of office to his officers of state, his conscience as regards the state accompanies them. No man in England, my Lords, is less disposed than I am to abridge the King's prerogative or degrade the dignity of his high office by reducing him to a cypher. The public, on the contrary, are entitled to a full benefit nay they have the right in reason to expect the advantages of the personal virtues and capacity of the King."

The King can command but he cannot perform and his commands are only valid if they are legal and given in legal form by being countersealed by a responsible officer of state. In consequence, every act of public authority and every exercise of power can be subject to Parliamentary scrutiny without involving the person of the King. Those who advise and those who consent, and those who perform any act of authority are directly responsible to Parliament in proceedings in which they cannot plead the commands of a superior.

How this was dealt with was shown in the trial of the Earl of Stafford who pleaded that he acted on the direct command of the King. In the trial as reported by Rushworth on Article 19, Mr. Whitlock, one of the managers of the House of Commons, declared:-

> "The committee (of the House of Commons) confess and think no man had ever yet heard to doubt, that the King would command anything that should be against the law; but it hath been sufficiently proved that my Lord of Stafford (A subordinate minister under the King) hath published his own commands in the King's name which are not justifiable nor according to law... and if my Lord of Stafford should procure a letter from his Majesty to do that which is not warrantable by law? The King's considerations are far above the particular points of the municipal law of the kingdom; he cannot know them, but is to be informed of them by ministers; now if my Lord of Stafford shall misinform him and to desire to have that by his authority which is not warrantable by law, the fault is my Lord of Stafford's and much aggravates the crime...."

> (Historical Collections, Vol. VIII, p. 509 The Trial of The Earl of Stafford)

Again Mr. Glyn, in reply to the Earl of Stafford's defence said on behalf of the House of Commons:-

> "My Lords. My Lord of Stafford doth very well know... that the King's servants are to serve him according to the law and not otherwise; he very well knew, that if an unlawful act be committed...the King's authority and warrant produced is no justification at all. So then, my Lords, to mention the King's name to justify an unlawful act in that way can do him no good and his own understanding knows it may do the King harm if

we had not so gracious a King that no such thing can do harm to...."

(Ibid, p. 730 (displaced)

This doctrine that the King can do no wrong has resulted in the constitutional position that the only personal prerogative of the crown, apart from the grant of honours, is the appointment to office. The prerogative of appointment to office, is however, not unconditional in that all those appointed must have skill and capacity in the professions to which they are appointed as otherwise the appointment is void. The skill and capacity of those appointed to offices of state and administration is subject to the continuous confidence of the House of Commons.

The constitutional position of the personal prerogative of the crown to appointment to office and the conditions surrounding this prerogative was re-affirmed on the defeat of George III in the resolution moved by Charles James Fox in the House of Commons and passed on March 8th 1784. This re-affirmed a cardinal principle of the English Parliamentary constitution in the following terms:-

> "To assure His Majesty, that we neither have disputed nor mean in any instant to dispute, much less to deny, his Majesty's undoubted prerogative of appointing to the executive offices of state such persons as to his Majesty's wisdom shall seem meet; but at the same time, that we must, with all humility, again submit to his Majesty's royal wisdom, that no administration, however legally appointed, can serve his Majesty and the public with effect, which does not enjoy the confidence of the House; and that in his Majesty's present administration we cannot confide; the circumstances under which it was constituted and the ground upon which it continues have created just suspicions in the breast of his faithful Commons that principles are adopted and views entertained unfriendly to the privileges of the House and to the freedom of our excellent constitution; that we have made no charge against them, because it is their removal not their punishment which we

have desired; and that we humbly conceive, we are
warranted by the ancient usage of this House, to desire
such removal without making any charge whatever;
that confidence may prudently be withheld where
no criminal process can be properly instituted...that
with regard to the propriety of admitting either the
present ministers or any other persons...it is a point
which we are too well acquainted with the bounds of
our duty to presume to offer any advice to his Majesty,
well knowing it to be the undoubted prerogative of his
Majesty to choose his ministers without any previous
advice from either House of Parliament and our duty
humbly to submit to his Majesty our advice when such
appointment shall appear to us to be prejudicial to the
public service."

(Parliamentary History of England Hansard, Vol. XXIV,
Col. 736)

Burke described this as the most noble and refined part of our
Parliamentary constitution. In "Present Discontents", he declared:-

"It has always been held to be the first duty of Parliament
to refuse to support government until power was in the
hand of persons who were acceptable to the people or
while factions predominated in the Court in which the
nation had no confidence. Thus all the good effects of
popular elections were supposed to be secured to us
without the mischiefs attending on perpetual intrigue
and a distinct canvas for every particular office through
the body of the people. This was the most noble and
refined part of our Constitution. The people by their
representatives and grandees were entrusted with the
deliberate power in making laws. The King with his
control of the negative. The King was entrusted with
the deliberate choice and the election of office, the
people had the negative in the Parliamentary refusal
to support. Formerly, this power of control was what
kept ministers in awe of Parliament and Parliament

in reverence of the people. If the use of this power of control in system and persons of administration is gone, everything is lost, Parliament and all.

(World Classics LXXI, Vol. 1, p. 57)

It is precisely this refined part of our Parliamentary heritage which the modern party cabinet system has totally undermined. With the membership of the House of Commons under party control, the party system can ensure that no confidence will be given to any appointment by the Crown however well qualified unless they are acceptable to the party managers.

The King is now compelled to accept party nominees whether qualified or not, and the highest patronage of the nation now falls into the exclusive control of the party managers. With the repeal of the Place clause in the Act of Settlement by the Regency Act of 1705, it is now open for the executive positions to be filled by members of the House of Commons, so that the majority parliamentary party is able to ensure that the highest positions of the state are filled by its own members.

To be elected the representative of the people is now the stepping stone to the highest and most powerful positions in the nation. To safeguard this position, the personal prerogatives of the Crown in the appointments to office have now to be exercised by "rules" that the party system has established. Sir Ivor Jennings, in his "Cabinet Government", gives us the nature of these rules:-

(1) The King's task is only to secure government, not to try to form a government which is likely to forward a policy of which he approved. (p. 28)

(2) Where the government is defeated and there is a leader of the Opposition, the King must send for him. The rule has for its corollary that before sending for the leader of the Opposition, the monarch should consult no one. If he takes advice first, it can only be for the purpose of keeping out the Opposition or its recognised leader. To try to keep out the Opposition is to take sides in a party issue. To try to defeat the claims of the recognised leader is to interfere in the internal affairs of the chief opposition party. (p. 48)

(3) The nomination of ministers rests with the Prime Minister...as against the King, the Prime Minister has the final word. He must have a government which can work together and which can secure the support of the House of Commons. If he says for this reason he must have the assistance of a certain person, the King must either give way or find another Prime Minister. The King cannot commission another member of the same party; for that is to interfere in the internal affairs of the party and is contrary to precedent; he must therefore find another party which can secure the support of the House of Commons, and it must be a strange House that is willing to support alternative governments. (p. 48)

Under the party system, the Crown cannot dismiss any Minister whatever he does, as under the doctrine of collective responsibility, the Minister by the party control of the House of Commons, can ensure that no alternative appointment would command the confidence of the House of Commons. The Crown is therefore put in the position that it is compelled to treat as a command the very humble advice these ministers choose to give. This power of dictation to the Crown is now claimed as the highest constitutional principle. But whereas those appointed to office by the Crown were responsible to an independent House of Commons over which the Crown had no control, those now appointed under the Party system are nominally responsible to a House of Commons completely under their own control. The great and crucial principle of ministerial responsibility to Parliament is now an empty fiction.

Professor Lowe, as long ago as 1904, in "The Governance of England", stated categorically that:-

"The House of Commons no longer controls the Executive; on the contrary, the Executive controls the House of Commons. The theory is, that the Ministers must justify each and all their acts before the representatives of the nation at every stage; if they fail to do so, those representatives will then turn them out of office. But in our modern practice, The Cabinet is scarcely turned out of office by Parliament whatever it does."

(Page 80)

Professor Ramsey Muir, in his evidence to the Select Committee on Procedure on Public Business in 1931, declared:-

> "There is no country in North Western Europe in which the control exercised by Parliament over the Government is more shadowy and unreal than it is in Britain. Parliament is no longer in any sense the sovereign power in the State."

(Commons Paper, 161 (1931))

The late Earl (at that time Mr.) Lloyd George, Prime Minister in the First World War and after, testifying before the same Committee on the question as to how Parliamentary control might be more effective, said:-

> "Well, it has no control. I am speaking now after forty years experience. Parliament has no control over the Executive; it is pure fiction."

(Ibid.)

How fictional it is can be seen in the words of Sir Ivor Jennings in "Cabinet Government", in which he tells us:-

> "Though it is true that the Government is responsible to the House of Commons, that must be understood in a peculiar sense."

(Page 16)

It must, in fact, be understood in the very peculiar sense that the very opposite is the truth, namely, that Government controls the House of Commons, for as Sir Ivor goes on to say:-

> "The House of Commons consists of parties. The Government as a party authority, has control over one or more of them. It appoints 'whips' and pays many of

them out of public funds. It is their function to see that the Members of the party attend the House and support the Government. If the Government hold together, the House does not control the Government, but the Government controls the House."

(Ibid p. 18)

We are today in the position described by Burke in "Present Discontents":-

"It must be always the wish of an unconstitutional statesman that a House of Commons, who are entirely dependent upon him, should have every right of the people entirely dependent on their pleasure. It was soon discovered that the forms of a free, and the ends of an arbitrary government were things not altogether incompatible...In Parliament, the power of obtaining their object is absolute; and the safety of the proceeding perfect; no rules to confine, no after reckoning to terrify. Parliament cannot, with any great authority, punish others for things in which they themselves have been accomplices. Thus the control of Parliament upon the executory power is lost because Parliament is made to partake of every considerable act of Government.

Impeachment, that great guardian of the purity of the Constitution is in danger of being lost even to the idea of it...

(Burke's italics)   (World Classics LXXI, Vol. 2, p. 11)

With the passing of the personal prerogative of the Crown in the appointment to office into the control of the party system, there has passed, too, the Royal Prerogative as the fountain of honour as well as the vast national patronage, including the secret service funds to be used for party purposes. This has a direct relationship to the House of Lords, not only as a co-ordinate institution of Parliament but also as the Supreme Court of English Law where constitutional issues alone can be finally determined.

In its judicial capacity, the House of Lords was a lay court, but it had the constitutional right to the advice of the whole bench of English judges in all issues arising in law and legislation. Before the downfall of the House of Lords as our Supreme Court, Chief Justice Hale in his work "The Jurisdiction of the Lords House of Parliament", written just before his death in 1676, tells us:-

> "He that considers the great reverence that hath been in all cases of law given to the resolution and opinion of the judges by the Lords in Parliament and how comfortable regularly the judgement of the Lords hath been to the opinion and advice of the judges upon matters of law transacted in the House of Lords...will find that though for many years past, they have only voices of advice and assistance, not authoritative or decisive; yet their opinions have been always the rules whereby the Lords do or should proceed in matters of law...unless the case be so momentous that they are not fit for the determination of judges, as in questions touching the right of succession of the Crown or the privileges of Parliament or the great cases that confirm the liberties and rights of the subject in general..."
>
> (The Jurisdiction of the Lords House of Parliament, Hale edited by Hargrave, 1796, p. 159)

The great part the lay members of the House of Lords played in the development of English Law was suggested by Lord Denning in his Romanes Lecture of 1959, "From Precedent to Precedent". Lord Denning then declared:-

> "I observe that in the past when the lawyers precedents have been found to work injustice, they have been corrected, as often as not, by the sections of juries or by the Lords of Parliament, who were for the most part, not lawyers."
>
> (From Precedent to Precedent, Lord Denning, Romanes Lecture, 1959)

Under the Party control, the Royal Prerogative was to be used not to the honour of the realm or to the benefit of the law and constitution, but almost entirely for Party ends and Party considerations including the sale of honours for the benefit of party funds.

The influence the party system has had on the House of Lords, especially in enlarging its hereditary aspect, can be seen in the growth of its membership. In 1688 at the time of the English Revolution, the membership was about 150, which included the non-hereditary spiritual peers. A century later, it had risen to about 294. By 1850 membership had reached 400. By 1959 it had reached to over 800. From 1880, when the party system had achieved complete supremacy, to 1920 - that is in the short period of forty years - no fewer than 453 peers were created. This is more than the total membership in 1850 which was already swollen as a result of party action. It was not till the 19th century, as H. R. Greaves points out in the " British Constitution", that the peers who held their seats by virtue of birth, seriously outnumbered those who had been ennobled for their services. This predominantly hereditary character of the House of Lords, on which the party system plays for its democratic appeal, springs directly from party action. It is an interesting fact that out of 453 peers created in the forty years from 1880 to 1920, no less than 259 were created by the Liberal Party which made " The Peers versus the People" one of the stock electioneering cries.

It is clear beyond any question that it is an abuse of the Royal Prerogative to create or threaten to create peers in order to force legislation through the House of Lords and thereby to destroy its equal co-ordinate standing as an institution of Parliament. The creation of peers for this purpose has only occurred once in our history, and on that single occasion, it was condemned by the House of Commons. The Minister who advised this action was impeached, and in their articles of impeachment, the House of Commons established the constitutional position on this issue. In these articles was included the following charge against Robert Harley, Earl of Oxford, when he was impeached in 1717:-

"...having on all occasions used his utmost endeavours to subvert the ancient established constitution of Parliament, the great and only security of the prerogative of the Crown and of the rights, liberties and properties of the people, and being most wickedly determined at one fatal blow as far as in him lay to destroy the freedom and independence of the House of Lords...did advise her Majesty to make and create twelve peers of this realm, and prevailed on her to exercise in the most unprecedented and dangerous manner that valuable and undoubted prerogative which the wisdom of the laws and constitution of this kingdom hath entrusted with the Crown for rewarding signal virtue with distinguished merit. By which desperate advice he did not only, as far as in him lay, deprive her Majesty on the continuance of those seasonable and wholesome counsels in that critical juncture, but wickedly perverted the true and only end of that great and useful prerogative to the dishonour of the Crown and the irreparable mischief to the constitution of Parliament."

(State Trials, Vol. 15, Col. 1082)

Though in this case this issue was not brought to conclusive judgement of the House of Lords, it remains a constitutional declaration of the House of Commons, which the Lords have not questioned.

It is true that in 1832 the threat of creating new peers was employed to force through the Reform Bill. Lord Brougham, one of the chief sponsors of the Bill, and Lord Chancellor in Lord Grey's administration, has left on record his opinion that rather than exercise this unconstitutional power, the Government might have dropped the Reform Bill itself. This is what Lord Brougham had to say in his book "The British Constitution":-

"In recent times the Government, of which I formed a part, backed by a large majority of the Commons and of the people out of doors, carried the Reform Bill through the Lords by the power which his late Majesty had conferred upon us of an unlimited creation of Peers at any stage of the measure. It was fortunate for the Constitution that the patriotism of the peers, acting under the sage counsels of the Duke of Wellington, prevented us from having recourse to a measure so full of peril. I have always regarded it as the greatest escape which I ever made in the whole course of my political

life...I have often asked myself the question, whether
or not, if no secession had taken place and the Peers
had persisted in really opposing the most important
provisions of the Bill, we should have had recourse
to the perilous creations? Well nigh thirty years have
rolled over my head since the crisis of 1832; I speak very
calmly of this, as on every political question whatever;
and I cannot with any confidence answer it in the
affirmative. When I went to Windsor with Lord Grey, I
had a list of eighty creations, framed upon the principle
of making the least permanent additions to our House,
and to the Aristocracy by calling up Peers eldest sons,
by choosing men without families; and by taking Scotch
and Irish Peers. I had a strong feeling of the necessity
of the case in the very peculiar circumstances we were
placed in. But such was my deep sense of the dreadful
consequence of the act, that I much question whether I
should not have preferred running the risk of confusion
that attended the loss of the Bill as it then stood; and I
have a strong impression on my mind that my illustrious
friend would have more than met me half way in the
determination to face that risk...rather than expose the
constitution to so imminent a hazard of subversion."

(Page 268)

The position of the House of Lords is now governed by some undefined
standard of "ethics". In the "Law of the Constitution," Dicey says:-

"The general rule that the House of Lords must,
in matters of legislation give way to the House of
Commons, is one of the best established maxims of
modern constitutional ethics. But if any enquirer asks
how the point at which the Peers are to give way is to
be determined, no answer which even approximates
to the truth, can be given except the very vague reply
that the Upper House must give way whenever it is
clearly proved that the will of the House of Commons
represents the deliberate will of the nation. On any

matters on which the electors are firmly resolved, a Premier who is, in effect, the representative of the House of Commons has the means of coercion, namely by the creation of Peers."

(8th edit., p. 454)

When in the course of time Dicey became the authority in the Conservative and Unionist opposition to the 1911 Parliament Bill, this passage made any effective opposition based upon constitutional grounds impossible. The Parliament Act is, in fact, nothing more than the expression of Dicey's statement for which, in the first place, he had no authority whatever.

A similar conception of "ethics" can be clearly seen in the sale of honours. This was declared illegal and condemned by the House of Commons when it impeached the Duke of Buckingham for high crimes. It is true that this issue never came to a final judgement of the House of Lords, owing to the dissolution of Parliament by Charles I in order to protect his favourites. It was never taken up again as Buckingham was murdered. In such circumstances, again, a declaration of the House of Commons must be accepted as a principle of constitutional law unless and until it has been reversed by the House of Lords. It requires no deep and subtle consideration to arrive at the conclusion that honour is a substance which cannot be bought or sold, and if a barony can be had for the payment of £40,000 to party funds, the title indeed may be had, but the honour which it implies is lost. The sale of honours is so flagrant an abuse and so repulsive in its character, that no constitutional authority would undertake its defence. It is one of those aspects of our modern political system which we hear very little. It is true that after the glaring scandals after the First World War, some machinery was established to minimise the evil, which has had a profound effect upon the moral standing of the House of Lords in the last century and a half. It has affected the standing of the House of Lords as our Supreme Court. Much as the Party system gained by the funds it obtained in this debauchery, it gained more by the destruction of the one court which might have and could have restrained its usurpation of the constitution.

Parliament today is nothing more than a purely technical co-ordination of a monarchy reduced to a constitutional cypher, a degraded and debased House of Lords, and a Party packed and marshalled House of Commons. It is this mockery of a supreme Parliament which is now vested with sovereignty above all law to which the people are now required to render passive obedience in the name of the Rule of Law.

THE PARTY CABINET AND THE DOCTRINE
OF CONSTITUTIONAL LAWLESSNESS

T he organ of Party Government is the Cabinet. The Cabinet is not and never has been a Parliamentary institution. Dicey, in his 1860 Arnold essay "The Privy Council," pointed out:-

> "The Cabinet is an anomaly, though it is one to which custom has made the present age so familiar, that its strangeness is forgotten. In theory the Cabinet is nothing but a committee of the Privy Council, yet with the council it has, in reality, no dealings and thus the extraordinary result has taken place that the government of England is in the hands of men whose position is legally undefined, and while the Cabinet is a word of every day use, no lawyer can say what a Cabinet is; that while no ordinary Englishman knows who the Lords of the Council are, the Church of England prays Sunday by Sunday that these Lords may be 'endowed with wisdom and understanding'. That while collective responsibility of ministers is a doctrine appealed to by members of the government, no less than by the opponents, it is more than doubtful whether such responsibility could be enforced by any legal penalties."

(Page 143)

In origin, the Cabinet Council was a prerogative device instituted by Charles II to defeat the principle of ministerial political responsibility to the House of Commons, the central issue raised by the Grand Remonstrance of 1641, the rejection of which, by Charles I, was a major factor that led to the Civil Wars. At the Restoration, this question was left open by tacit consent, neither King nor Parliament altering their position. To ensure that the issue would not again be brought to a head, Charles II adopted the practice of holding secret meetings of selected ministers at which decisions on policy and administration were taken and then confirmed at a formal meeting of the Privy Council, as the legal executive body. By collective action and under conditions of secrecy, it became difficult, if not impossible, for the House of Commons to discover which Minister could be held responsible for any action or policy, or even to know what advice had been given to the Crown. Hallam, in his "Constitutional History of England", gives a footnote quoting Trenchard's "Short History of Standing Armies", which clearly shows the constitutional implications that were involved. This extract reads:-

> "Formerly all matters of State and discretion were debated and resolved in the Privy Council, where every man subscribed his opinion and was answerable for it. The late King Charles II was the first who broke this most excellent part of our Constitution, by setting up a cabal or cabinet council, where all matters of consequence were debated and resolved, and then brought to the Privy Council to be confirmed."
>
> (8th edit. 1867, Vol. 3, p, 183)

Hallam brings out the significance of the growth of Cabinet Government when he writes:-

> "During the reign of William III, this distinction of the Cabinet from the Privy Council and the exclusion of the latter from all business of State became more fully established. This, however, produced a serious consequence, as to the responsibility of the advisers of the Crown and at the very time when the controlling and chastising power of Parliament was most effectually recognised, it was silently eluded by the concealment in which the objects of its enquiry would wrap themselves."
>
> (8th edit., 1867, Vol.3, p. 183)

The existence of the Cabinet constituted a serious threat to the Constitution in that it made the exercise of the Royal Prerogative independent from effective parliamentary control. To meet this situation, the Act of Settlement of 1701 included a clause aimed to stamp out the Cabinet development. This clause read:-

> "All matters and things relating to the well governing of this Kingdom which are properly recognisable in the Privy Council by the laws and customs of this realm shall be transacted there and all resolutions taken thereon shall be signed by such of the Privy Council as shall advise and consent to the same."

(The Statutes Revised, 2nd edit., p. 761)

To preserve the purity of popular representation, there also was included in the Act of Settlement the prohibition against any elected representative being appointed to or holding any office in government or administration, which read as follows:-

> "No person who has an office or place of profit under the King or received a pension from the Crown shall be capable of serving as a member of the House of Commons."

(Ibid)

These two clauses in the Act of Settlement were repealed by the Regency Act of 1705 before they came into operation. England at that date was at war with France, which was supporting the Stuart Pretender at a time when Scotland, before the union with England, was in a hostile mood and inclined to reject the English settlement for the succession of the Crown. Queen Anne refused to have her heirs from Germany residing in this country with the result that if she suddenly died, the Pretender would be less than three days journey distant to land in Scotland with the heir to the English throne more than six weeks journey distant. To overcome this period, the Regency Act provided for a council to be set up and for the continuation of Parliament and the Privy Council and other appointments for a period of six months. As members of the House of Commons already acted in offices appointed by the Crown, their forced retirement in such a critical time would create an unnecessary confusion. Further, the new regency council would have to work with the Privy Council, which the clause in the act of settlement might seriously hamper. It was felt, too, that with members of the House of Commons being appointed to the cabinet council, the constitutional objection to this body was to some extent overcome. Thus purely for temporary reasons, a fundamental change in the English constitution was initiated, the consequences of which are with us today. The Regency Act provided a negative legal sanction to the very abuses which the two repealed clauses were intended to prevent and opened the way to the corruption of Parliament by Cabinet Government, first by George III in the early years of his reign and finally by the party system of today.

The outstanding feature of the Cabinet is that nothing is known about it and that it exercises its authority in absolute secrecy, now strongly enforced by the Official Secrets Act. This quality of secrecy was brought out by Walter Bagehot in "The English Constitution," in which he points out that:-

> "The most curious point about the Cabinet is that so very little is known about it. The meetings are not only secret in theory, but secret in reality...The Committee which unites the law-making power and the law executing power which by virtue of that combination is, while it lasts and holds together, the most powerful body in the state, is a committee wholly secret."
>
> (World Classics CCCXXX, p.286)

In the introduction to the second edition, Bagehot reverted to the same theme:-

> "No one would venture to suggest that a committee of Parliament on Foreign Relations should be able to commit the country to the greatest international obligations without consulting either Parliament or the country. No other select committee has any comparable power; and considering how carefully we have fettered and limited the powers of all other subordinate authorities, our allowing so much discretionary power on matters peculiarly dangerous and peculiarly delicate to rest on the sole charge of one secret committee is exceedingly strange. No doubt it may be beneficial;

many seeming anomalies are so, but at first sight it does not look right"

(Page 286)

A former Lord Rosebery, who had himself been Prime Minister, in his chapter on "Sir Robert Peel" included in his "Miscellanies Literary and Historical," also remarked on the strange spectacle of secret government when he said:-

"Nothing is indeed more remarkable than the cohesion of Cabinets, except that strange institution itself. To the Briton who found it existing at his birth, it seems the natural if not the inevitable form of government. To the enquiring foreigner, however, nothing can seem more extraordinary, in a country with so much of democracy about it, than the spectacle of a secret council, on the Venetian model, and sworn to absolute silence, conducting the business of a nation which insists on publicity for everything less important. The secrecy of the Cabinet in such a condition of things would resemble, one would surmise, the secrecy of the ostrich - the material fact would be visible to all while a shallow head was embedded in the sand. But it is not so . The secrets of the Cabinet are as a rule preserved. After the sharpest internal discords the members will present a united, even if a silent and sullen, front. Whether the system of Cabinet government be an efficient one or not is not now the question; whether the collection of the heads of departments at sparse intervals to discuss hurriedly topics, for which they are often unprepared, be a good arrangement for business is not the point ; but what may confidently be asserted is that of all anomalous arrangements for executive government in an Anglo-Saxon community during the present epoch and under the present conditions, the strangest is the government of the British Empire by a secret committee."

(Page 202)

It is Sidney Low, in "The Governance of England," first published in 1904, who, more clearly than any other constitutional authority, describes the secrecy of the Cabinet. He writes:-

> "The fact that the English Cabinet is a secret committee is in reality a most astonishing phenomenon, though use and wont have obscured its significance to our eyes. We have been so familiar with it for generations that we often forget its peculiarity. We take it as a matter of course that the gravest concerns of a people among whom publicity and public discussion prevail to an extent seldom equalled, should be decided under a cloak of impenetrable darkness. The cabinet is a secret, not a private, Committee. The distinction is essential, though often overlooked. Most Englishmen are aware that the Cabinet meets in private; few of them have perhaps realised that it sits and works in secrecy. In this respect it stands apart from nearly all governing councils, in ancient and modern times, as well as from most other boards of management. Privacy is not unusual. It is indeed an element of the committee system...Business cannot properly be transacted at a public meeting. But though a good committee takes care to obtain the advantages of privacy it is not as a rule permitted to assert the further prerogative of secrecy... The Cabinet has carried secrecy and informality to the highest pitch. Its meetings are still supposed to be nothing but casual consultations between a number of Privy Councillors."

(Page 34)

The first to take note of the fact that the new Party Cabinet represented principles of law and government diametrically opposed to those of the English Parliamentary constitution was Walter Bagehot in "The English Constitution", first published in 1867. At that time, the constitutional authority was Blackstone's "Commentaries on the Laws of England", as brought up to date and re-arranged by James Stephen. In 1868 in the sixth edition of his re-arrangement of Blackstone, Sergeant Stephen repeated the same words of Blackstone written one hundred years ago as to the nature of our constitution, which read:-

> "In all tyrannical governments the supreme magistracy or the right both of making or enforcing laws, is vested in one and the same man or one and the same body of men and whenever these two powers are united together there can be no public liberty. The magistrate may enact tyrannical laws, and execute them in a tyrannical manner, since he is possessed in quality of dispenser of justice with all the power which he as legislator, thinks proper to give himself. But where the legislative and executive authority are in distinct hands, the former will take care not to entrust the latter with so large a power, as may tend to the subversion of its own independence, and therewith the liberty of the subject. With us, therefore, in England, this supreme power is divided into two branches; the legislative to wit, the Parliament consisting of King, Lords and Commons, and the other, the executive consisting of the King alone."

> (Blackstone, Ch. 2, P. 146 and Stephen's "New Commentaries", 6th edit., 1868, Book IV, Ch. 1, p. 342)

Bagehot, however, pointed out that what he called the English Constitution rested on totally opposite principles. He declared that:-

> "The efficient secret of the English Constitution may be described as the close union, the nearly complete fusion of the executive and legislative powers. No doubt by the traditional theory as it exists in all books, the goodness of our constitution consists of the entire separation of the legislative and executive authorities but in truth its merit consists in their singular approximation. The connecting link is the Cabinet. By that new word we mean a committee of the legislative body selected to be the executive body."

> (World Classics, CCCXXX, p. 9)

Walter Bagehot himself had no legal or constitutional standing, and the whole system of the Party Cabinet government was open to challenge on constitutional grounds. This was finally resolved by A. V. Dicey, who, as Professor of English Law at the University of Oxford, published in 1885 his "Lectures Introductory to the study of the law of the Constitution", now known as Dicey's "Law of the Constitution" in which he gave not only the Party Cabinet system but the whole corruption of Parliament a constitutional form. Dicey's achievement rested on the fact that he wrote not like Bagehot as a commentator but as an English lawyer.

As Professor Wade remarked in his introduction to the tenth edition of the "Law of the Constitution":-

> "It may be said of Dicey that his continuing influence on the study of the constitution would have been less enduring if he had not written primarily as a lawyer."

(Page XX)

Dicey's "Law of the Constitution" is an astonishing phenomenon in that Dicey enjoys the unique distinction of being his own authority in defiance of all other authorities, whether custom, precedent, and even Parliamentary legislation. In his works, Dicey defies not only a thousand years of unbroken legal development but even the very principles of constitutional law which he himself has laid down. Dicey became increasingly aware of the inherent contradictions in his work. These he expressed in later writings, particularly in his introduction to the eighth edition of the "Law of the Constitution". This, however, did not counterbalance the authority of his original work, which he refused to retract or re-write.

Since 1885 Dicey's work has passed through ten editions with thirteen reprints but is basically unaltered since it first appeared. The eighth edition appeared in 1915 and was the last in Dicey's lifetime and included a long introduction by Dicey himself. The ninth edition appeared in 1939 and the tenth in 1959, in both of which Dicey's introduction was replaced by equally long ones by Professor E. C. S. Wade. It can be no exaggeration to say that Dicey's "Law of the Constitution" has been the dominant factor in English Constitutional development for over eighty years. It remains to this day as the primary authority of our modern political system.

Dicey's central theme is the doctrine of the sovereignty of Parliament, with which he replaced the central constitutional principle of the legal supremacy of Parliament. In the "Law of the Constitution," he declared that:-

> "The sovereignty of Parliament is (from a legal point of view) the dominant characteristic of our political institutions."

> (10th edit., P. 39)

Or alternatively:-

> "The one fundamental dogma of English Constitutional Law is the absolute legislative sovereignty or despotism of the King in Parliament."

> (10th edit., p. 145)

In the English Parliamentary constitution this doctrine had no foundation whatsoever.

As Professor Wade has put it, rather mildly, in his introduction to the ninth edition of Dicey's "Law of the Constitution":-

> "Dicey does not cite any decision in support of his classic exposition of the sovereignty of Parliament. His jurisprudence is the Austinian theory of law as a command. But it is doubtful whether the British Constitution does contain an illustration of a sovereign as the sole source of authority."

> (Page XXXVIII)

Dicey nevertheless insisted in defiance of Austin himself (see Appendix) that:-

> "Sovereignty, like many of Austin's conceptions, is a generalisation drawn in the main from English Law - in England we are accustomed to the existence of a supreme legislative body, i.e., a body which can make or unmake every law, the true conception of a sovereign

and the case with which the theory of absolute
sovereignty has been accepted by English jurists is due
to the peculiar history of English Constitutional Law."

(10th edit., p. 72)

The full implication of Austin's theory of sovereignty as applied by Dicey to the English Parliament can only be fully understood by an examination of Austin's own position.

John Austin was a lecturer on jurisprudence at the newly formed University of London just prior to the passing of the Reform Act of 1832, and his legal conceptions were propounded in his lectures, published under the title of "The Province of Jurisprudence Determined".

Austin had failed at the English Bar and took up the lectureship as an alternative means of livelihood. In preparing for his lectures, he turned not to English centres of legal study but to the German universities, which had for centuries been active in the study of Roman Law in its original and revived forms. At the time he was in Germany, academic legal activity was directed to the creating of a new code in the place of that which the Napoleonic occupation had left behind. In this activity, there was already clearly visible the totalitarian sentiments which were to reach supremacy under the Nazi party dictatorship.

The essential principles of Austin's jurisprudence were derived from the Roman Civil Law, which he regarded as greater and palpably superior to the Law of England. He declared:-

"Turning from the study of the English to the study of
the Roman Law, you escape from the empire of chaos
and darkness to a world which seems by comparison,
the region of order and light."

(2nd edit. P. LCIV)

Austin insisted that all law was the command of the supreme authority which exists in every independent political community. When it is not this, he claimed, it is not law at all. He may be quoted thus:-

"Every positive law or every law simply and strictly so
called is set by a sovereign person or a sovereign body

of persons to the members of the independent political society wherein that person or body is sovereign or supreme or (changing the expression) it is set by a monarch or sovereign member to a person or persons in a state of subjection to its author. Even though it sprung directly from another fountain or source, it is positive law or a law strictly so called by the institution of that present sovereign in the character of political superior, or , (borrowing the language of Hobbes) "The legislator is he, not by whose authority the law was first made but by whose authority it continues to be law."

(Ibid. p. 118 & 169)

It is not necessary to enter into the dreary wastes of intellectual speculation which Austinian jurisprudence opens and to which there can be no finality. It is only necessary to recognise the fundamental issue which this jurisprudence raised in the total destruction of all constitutional law in relation to the sovereign authority. The law, according to Austin, is the will of the sovereign and the sovereign cannot, therefore, be bound by law. On this point, he says:-

"Monarchs and sovereign bodies have attempted to oblige themselves, or to oblige the successors to their sovereign powers. But in spite of the laws which sovereigns have imposed upon themselves or which they have imposed upon the successors to their sovereign powers, the position that sovereign power is incapable of legal limitation will hold universally and without exception."

(Province of Jurisprudence determined 2nd edit., p. 226)

Under the Austinian theory of sovereignty, what goes under the name of constitutional law is, in fact, only constitutional "morality" and therefore, any practice of the constitution, however otherwise illegal, can be described as constitutional law. In the words of Austin:-

"Against a monarch properly so called or against a sovereign body in its collegiate or sovereign capacity, constitutional law is positive morality merely, or is enforced merely by moral sanctions. Whether constitutional law has been expressly adopted or simply consists of principles current in the political community, it is merely guarded against the sovereign by sentiments or feelings of the governed. Consequently, although an act of sovereignty which violates constitutional law may be styled with propriety unconstitutional, it is not an infringement of law simply or strictly so called and cannot be styled with propriety illegal"

(ibid. p. 230)

The clear and definite conclusion to be drawn from Austin's theory of sovereignty is that there is no constitutional law which can control or bind or define the sovereign.

The effect of the doctrine of Parliamentary sovereignty is to invalidate all constitutional law with the consequence that what was constitutional in law now becomes unconstitutional in practice, and practices have to be accepted as constitutional however flagrantly illegal.

In applying Austinian sovereignty to Parliament, Dicey was, in effect, declaring that the one fundamental law of the English Constitution is that there is no constitutional law whatsoever - not even the law which defines Parliament. Dicey disguised this by defining Parliamentary sovereignty in terms of Parliamentary supremacy.

He declared that:-

"Parliament means in the mouth of a lawyer ...the King, the House of Lords and the House of Commons; these three bodies acting together may be aptly described as the 'King in Parliament' and constitutes Parliament.

The principle of Parliamentary sovereignty means neither more nor less than this, namely that Parliament so defined has under the English Constitution, the right to make or unmake any law whatever and further, that no person or body is recognised by the law of England as having a right to override or set aside the legislation of Parliament."

(10th edit. p. 39)

Such a definition of Parliamentary sovereignty, however, cannot be reconciled with Austinian sovereignty, which Dicey was purporting to apply.

As Eastwood and Keeton point out in their textbook "The Austinian Theories of Law and Sovereignty":-

"A rule which at one time was a great favourite with Austin's critics is the rule that an English Statute can only be made by the King, the House of Lords and the House of Commons ...The truth is that the rule in question is a convention, a maxim of constitutional morality not a law."

(Page 25)

This raises the issue which still troubles the Austinian school.

As Professor Hart, in his introduction to the "Library of Ideas" edition of Austin's "Province of Jurisprudence Determined" puts it:-

"Those who have been agonised by the question 'How can a fundamental constitutional law be law?' might be content when it is shown that a defining characteristic of a legal system just is that it includes a fundamental rule for the identification of the other rules of the system. But, of course, all this would be an amendment of Austin, and not as some have suggested what he "really" meant."

That Dicey meant what Austin meant is shown by his emphatic statement that:-

"There is under the English Constitution no marked or clear distinction between laws which are not fundamental or constitutional and laws which are fundamental or constitutional."

(10th edit. P. 89)

81

Then why give a fundamental definition of Parliament as Lawyers define Parliament?

Dicey, as an English lawyer, could not deny the existence of fundamental constitutional law, but as an Austinian, he is compelled to do so. He, therefore, takes refuge in an impossible proposition, namely that constitutional law includes both lawful law and lawless law!

Dicey declared that:-

> "Constitutional law...consists of two elements. The one element here called the "Law of the Constitution" is a body of undoubted law, the other element here called the conventions of the constitution consists of maxims or practices..are not in strictness laws at all."

> (10th edit., p.24)

In another passage, however, Dicey questions whether what he himself described as "undoubted" law is, in fact law when he wrote:-

> "It is certain that understandings are not laws and that no system of conventionalism will explain the whole nature of constitutional law, if indeed constitutional law be in strictness law at all"

> (10th edit., p. 21)

To support this case, Dicey relied on a quotation from the work of the historian Freeman when he wrote:-

> "We have now a whole system of political morality, a whole code of precepts for the guidance of public men, which will not be found in any page of either the Statute Book or the Common Law, but which are in practice, held hardly less sacred than any principle embodied in the Great Charter or the Petition of Right. In short, by the side of our written law has grown up an unwritten or conventional constitution. When an Englishman speaks of the conduct of a public man being constitutional or

unconstitutional, he means something wholly different from what he means by conduct being legal or illegal."

(Law of the Constitution, 10th edit., p. 418)

It is, however, to be noted how little weight this "written" law of our constitution carries with Dicey, whose work is known as the Law of the Constitution. Nowhere in the whole work does Dicey discuss, if indeed he deigns to mention, this "written" law of our constitution which he should recognise as true law, having the weight of Parliamentary enactment behind it. The constitutional enactments of Parliament are, however, ignored by Dicey. Magna Carta itself is deemed worthy of no more than a single off-hand reference, though, according to Coke, confirmed by Parliament over thirty times. The Bill of Rights, the nearest thing we have to a constitutional code standing in our Statute Book, is only just mentioned. Dicey is so preoccupied with what he himself called the Conventions of the Constitution, that he is clearly more concerned with justifying the conventions of the constitution as the basis of our constitutional system than he is with the re-affirmation of the true law of the Constitution.

Dicey attempts to reconcile the conventions of the Constitution with his definition of Parliamentary sovereignty by making it appear as if the conventions of the constitution are nothing more than the variations of legal practice. He does this by claiming that the English Constitution is "flexible" not by virtue of the conventions but by Parliamentary enactment and thus differs from the "rigid" type of constitution such as the American. On this score, Dicey writes:-

"A flexible constitution is one under which every law of every description can be legally changed with the same ease and in the same manner by one and the same body. The flexibility of our constitution consists in the right of the Crown and the two houses (of Parliament) to modify or repeal any law whatever ...With us, laws, therefore are called constitutional because they refer to subjects supposed to affect the fundamental institutions of the State, and not because they are legally more sacred or difficult to change than any other laws and as a matter of fact the meaning of the words 'constitutional law or enactment' is rarely applied to any English statute as giving a definite description of its character. A 'rigid' constitution is one under which certain laws generally known as constitutional or fundamental laws cannot be changed in the same manner as ordinary laws."

(Law of the Constitution, 10th edit., p.127)

According to this, the distinction between "flexible" and "rigid" constitutions is a difference in the legislative processes, but Dicey goes on to say:-

"In some instances, that fact that certain laws or institutions of a state have been marked off as placed beyond the sphere of political controversy has apparently prevented that process of gradual innovation which in England has within not much more than sixty years transformed our polity...the Constitution of the United States has lasted for more than a hundred years but has not undergone anything like the amount of change which has been experienced by the constitution of England since the death of George III."

(10th edit., p.128)

The fact is that at the same time as these words were written there had been, and to a large extent there has still been, virtually no change in English constitutional law since the reign of George III. Any examination of the legal structure of our constitution reveals that our constitutional law is practically the same today as it was two or more hundred years ago and that, in law, the English constitution is as rigid as the American constitution. This is borne out by Dicey's assertion in 1912 when he declared:-

"Till 1867, or rather till 1884, Englishmen and Parliament on the whole practically accepted the unchangeableness of the Constitution."

(Rights of Citizenship, p. 84)

The fact, however, remains that our political system has undergone a complete transformation achieved not by legislation as constitutional "flexibility" would suggest but solely by the constitutional conventions.

Since Dicey's "Law of the Constitution," we are left with a sovereign Parliament and no constitutional law. As Sir Ivor Jennings, in his textbook "Law and the Constitution" points out:-

> "Strictly speaking, there is no constitutional law at all in Great Britain. There is only the arbitrary power of Parliament."
>
> (2nd edit., p. 64)

But this arbitrary power of Parliament in matters constitutional is expressed not by legislation but solely by the constitutional conventions. Under Austinian sovereignty, conventions of the constitution assume the quality of law though never enacted by Parliament. They have the force of law merely because Parliament has permitted them, and one has to presume that what a sovereign permit's, the sovereign has commanded though no written record of the command can be produced, or as Austin put it, they represent a "tacit" command (neither written nor spoken) of the sovereign.

In their textbook "The Austinian Theories of Law and Sovereignty," R. A. Eastwood and G. W. Keeton declare:-

> "It is said that the nature of the Conventions of the Constitution is such that they cannot be refused the name of law in any practical mind"
>
> (Page 23)

These conventions are now virtually the law of the constitution and their fickle unprincipled instability can be judged from the very nature of the conventions themselves.

Professor Berriedale Keith, in his work "The British Cabinet System 1830-1939", tells us that:-

> "Conventions are merely usages and they are styled conventions without any implications that they have the force of law. In the case of conventions it is always possible to argue that it is not established that what has happened in the past is not a binding precedent and that in the new circumstances a new line should be struck

out. This position is aided by the fact that while writers of text books on constitutional matters seldom disagree as to the law, they do disagree in the most marked manner as to the extent to which conventions exist and are binding and their views necessarily change with each practical issue."

(Page 6)

Professor Wade, in his introduction to the ninth (and tenth) edition of Dicey's "Law of the Constitution," tells us that:-

"The reason why conventions are obeyed may be obscure just as their actual operation is a mystery too deep to be fathomed by the lawyer, but the fact that Cabinet Government and the whole administrative machine only function effectively by these means, must be acknowledged."

(10th edit., p. CXCVII)

There is, however, no mystery. With the elimination of constitutional law by the doctrine of Parliamentary sovereignty, the Party system has liberated itself from all constitutional restraint.

No matter how widely the parties may appear to be divided on other issues, they always unite in fierce defence of their power, prerogatives and privileges which they have established by the constitutional conventions. Any attempt to regulate or control this power which all parties now claim to be "constitutional" will be resisted to the utmost. The conventions of the constitution are, in fact, nothing more than the agreements and understandings of the party organisations as to how they may exercise the supreme authority outside the law of the constitution. As Sir Ivor Jennings has put it in his "Law and the Constitution":-

"The conventions are a mere matter of practice though recognised as obligatory and are enshrined, so to speak, in the hearts of members and party officials."

(2nd edit., p. 112)

The conventions of the constitution, which are now the law of the constitution, are determined by nothing more than the ever changing demands of political party activity.

The English Constitution, which has stood like a rock for a thousand years as the greatest system of free government in the history of mankind, is now, by the operation of the constitutional conventions, reduced to a state of constant flux.

In the 1935 edition of his "Cabinet Government", Sir Ivor Jennings in his introduction, records that:-

> "The British Constitution is changing so rapidly that it is difficult to keep pace with it."

The changes are achieved in absolute secrecy by Cabinet practices for as Sir Ivor, in the same introduction, pointed out:-

> "The most important parts of the Cabinet system function is secret. Information is rarely made available until the persons concerned in particular events are dead. The constitutional lawyer is apt, therefore, to be a generation behind the times."

The people of England do not know, and they do not need to be informed as to the operations of the party system, which now absolutely controls their national destiny and welfare.

Such is the constitutional basis of the Party Cabinet system. By the simple but confusing process of declaring that the legal supremacy of Parliament vests Parliament with a sovereignty above all law, Dicey has given legal force to anything which a party packed Parliament has given a tacit consent under the name of constitutional conventions and thus legalises any practice of the party system and its Cabinet institution. Dicey did not have to discuss the Cabinet. He refers to it as a committee as if it had full constitutional standing. He gave full constitutional endorsement to Bagehot's "The English Constitution" though it carried no legal authority whatsoever. In the "Law of the Constitution," Dicey declared that:-

> "Bagehot was the first author who explained in accordance with actual facts the true nature of the Cabinet and its real relation to Crown and to Parliament.

He is in short one of those rare teachers who have explained intricate matters with such complete clearness as to make the public forget that what is now so clear ever needed explanation"

(10th edit., p. 19)

But in his Arnold essay "The Privy Council," Dicey made it clear that the cabinet is not and never has been a constitutional institution.

Dicey's sole justification for the constitutional conventions was on the ground that they adapted the Parliamentary constitution to meet democratic requirement. He covered this by asserting that:-

"The fundamental dogma of modern constitutionalism is that the legal sovereignty of Parliament is subordinate to the political sovereignty of the nation."

(10th edit., p. 453)

Dicey claimed that the achievement of this aim was the great accomplishment of the constitutional transformation of the past hundred years. As he put it in "The Law of the Constitution":-

"We may assert that the arrangements of the Constitution are now such as to ensure that the will of the electors shall by regular and constitutional means, always in the end assert itself as the predominant influence in the country. But this is a political and not a legal fact. The electors can in the long run always enforce their will."

(10th edit., p. 73)

According to Dicey, the end and purpose of the constitutional conventions:-

"...is to secure that Parliament or the Cabinet which is indirectly appointed by Parliament, shall in the long run, give effect to the will of the power which in modern England is the true political sovereignty of (to use a popular, though not quite accurate language) the Nation."

(10th edit., p. 429)

Dicey further insisted that:-

> "Neither the Crown nor any of the servants of the Crown ever refuses obedience to the grand principle which ...underlies the conventional precepts of the constitution, namely, that the Government must be carried on in accordance with the will of the House of Commons and ultimately with the will of the nation as expressed through that house." (10th edit., p. 442)

On the same grounds, Dicey justified the changes in the constitution of Parliament itself by constitutional conventions. As Dicey laid it down in "The Law of the Constitution":-

> "The conduct of the legislature which (ex hypothesi) cannot be governed by laws should be regulated by understandings of which the object is to secure the conformity of Parliament to the will of the nation. And this is what has actually occurred. The conventions of the constitution now consists of customs which are at the present day maintained for the sake of ensuring the supremacy of the House of Commons and ultimately, through the elective House of Commons, of the nation."

(10th edit., p. 430)

This convention strikes at the very root of Parliamentary supremacy and even at Dicey's own definition of Parliamentary sovereignty. In form, it makes the modern Parliament the same as the Cromwellian Parliaments of three centuries ago and which have ever since 1660 been denounced as illegal.

What is more, these conventions of the constitution have not achieved the only purpose for which they were justified by Dicey, namely to ensure that the will of the people shall prevail in national affairs, but only to ensure the supremacy of the Party Cabinet.

Dicey pointed out in his introduction to the 8th (1915) edition of "The Law of the Constitution" in answer to the question as to the general tendency of the constitutional conventions, that:-

> "It is assuredly to increase the power of any party which possesses a parliamentary majority, i.e. a majority, however got together, of the House of Commons and finally to place the control of legislation and indeed the whole government of the country, in the hands of the Cabinet which is in England at once the instrument through which a dominant party can exercise its power, and the only body in the State which can lead and control the parliamentary majority of which the cabinet is the organ. That the rigidity and strength of the party system or (to use an American expression) of the machine, has continued with every successive generation to increase in England, is the conviction of the men who have most thoroughly analysed the English political institutions as they exist and work..."

> (Page LV)

Sir Ivor Jennings pointed out in the "The Law and the Constitution" that:-

> "..most of the Conventions relate to the operation of the party system, which is merely an aspect of Cabinet Government. The principles governing the working of that system have never been formally recognised by Parliament or the Courts. As far as the Courts are concerned, they developed too late. The principle of constitutional law established by the Courts recognises the constitution of the Revolution settlement. Institutions and practices which have grown up since that time have not received the formal recognition by the Courts, and the rules relating to them are not part of Common Law. Accordingly the rules relating to the foundation and operation of the Cabinet, the relations between Prime Minister and other Ministers, between the Government and Opposition, and many more are

not in legislation, nor in the Common Law nor in the law and custom of Parliament."

(2nd edit., p.112)

Sir Ivor Jennings points out in "Cabinet Government" that:-

"The whole system of Cabinet Government is founded not on laws, but on practices. This does not mean that the existence of the most important constitutional authorities is contrary to law. It means only that they are not recognised by law."

(Page 2)

Whatever Dicey may have professed in his main work as the justification of the constitutional conventions to make effective the will of the nation, thirty years later, he had to record a totally different conclusion. In the introduction to the 8th (1915) edition of "The Law of the Constitution," he wrote:-

"The Cabinet ...can defy on matters of the highest importance, the possible or certain will of the nation. This growth of the authority obtained by the men who can control the party machine is more formidable if we adopt the view propounded by the ablest critics of the Government of England and hold with Lovell that Party government has been for generations, not the accident or the corruption but, so to speak, the very foundation of our constitutional system."

(Page C)

The Party Cabinet now represents a concentration of power such as has never been tolerated previously in the whole of English history. Never before has national authority been so irresponsibly exercised with such impunity as now. As Professor Ramsey Muir put it in "How Britain is Governed":-

"In monopolising all power, the Cabinet has loaded itself with more work than it can do, and like all despots it is apt to be jealous of any attempt to reduce its powers... The Cabinet has arrogated to itself half blindly a series of colossal responsibilities which it cannot meet, which it will not allow Parliament to tackle, and which are not met at all except in so far as they are assumed by the bureaucracy behind the cloak of Cabinet omnipotence."

(pp. 102, 105)

As Professor Wade points out in his introduction to the tenth edition of Dicey's "Law of the Constitution":-

"It is the Cabinet system which is fundamental to Parliamentary Government. This system depends upon its efficiency as an instrument of government upon being able to use the legal supremacy of Parliament (or rather of the Commons) to serve its ends; it is saved from being an autocratic instrument by the knowledge that at intervals the electorate may alter the composition of the Commons and so place the supremacy of Parliament in other hands. But it is the political supremacy rather than the legal doctrine which saves the democratic principle. Indeed the legal instrument of Parliamentary supremacy stands in some risk of actually facilitating the creation of an extreme form of government at the present time, since all change however fundamental can be accomplished in law by any ordinary enactment of Parliament."

(Page CXCIV)

The fact is that Dicey's doctrine of Parliamentary sovereignty is a constitutional monstrosity by which the legal supremacy of Parliament has been reduced to an empty legal fiction.

Professor Wade, in his introduction to the ninth edition of Dicey's "Law and the Constitution," in which the doctrine of Parliamentary sovereignty is maintained in all its original force, writes:-

"The political supremacy of Parliament as a law-making organ becomes more and more fiction. Legislation is a compromise of conflicting interests. Parliament can no longer compel save in outward form."

(Page XLIV)

We see this fiction of Parliamentary supremacy in Keith's seventh edition of Ridge's "Constitutional Law of England." On page 16 of that work, we are told that:-

"The sovereignty or omnipotence of Parliament means that Parliament is the supreme power in the State."

But on the page immediately preceding this statement, there is a paragraph headed "Executive Control of Parliament."

(Page 15)

In their work, "Constitutional Law," the joint authors, E.G. Wade and G. Godfrey Phillips, point out:-

"It does not serve any useful purpose in emphasising the supremacy of Parliament in law without drawing attention to the many limitations by which it is restricted in fact. While there is no doubt that the form of law making is preserved as a necessary function of Parliament, it is not unreasonable to assert that the form is utilised almost exclusively by the Government of the day, with which rests the political supremacy to give effect to its policy. Thus the co-operation between Government and Parliament (or rather the House of Commons) involves a partnership in which the former rules and the latter, with occasional protests, confirm the senior partner's decision by formal approval."

(Page 59)

Not the sovereign Parliament but the anti-constitutional and secret Party Cabinet is now the supreme authority of the English nation.

As Sir Ivor Jennings put it in the opening sentence of the first chapter of "Cabinet Government:-

> "The Cabinet is the core of the British Constitutional system. It is the supreme directing authority."

Before the outbreak of the first world war in 1914 already there was a growing concern at the direction of English constitutional developments. In the political literature of that time, the Party system is referred to as a tawdry sham and questions were raised as to whether the true issue that faced the English people was not the People versus the Peers, which then filled the political stage, but rather the People versus the Party System. Among many others, we have the trenchant views expressed in 1912 by the Rt. Hon. F. E. Smith, K.C., M. P., later to be a great Lord Chancellor under the title of the Earl of Birkenhead, when he wrote :-

> "There is much to be said for a democratic system of government, as there is much to be urged on behalf of an autocratic. There is nothing whatever that can be urged in favour of a constitution which under the name of democracy, has in effect concentrated every faculty of government in the hands of a very small clique which has cheated the people of every vestige of effective control over national policy...who is it who governs England with unrestricted power, controlled by no checks or balances, and able to write his or their will on all subjects upon the pages of the Statute Book? The legatees of the people, the Lords and the Commons, are the cabinet of the day... Whether the people like their new constitution remains to be seen, but if they do and are prepared to stereotype it, they may have many merits but they will have ceased to be democrats."

(Rights of Citizenship, Ch. 2 pp. 27&36)

The outbreak of the First World War and the problems it brought in the social and industrial life of the nation created a constitutional apathy in which the Party Cabinet system was able to bed itself in, and the system it represented, in fact became stereotyped. This apathy was, however, to some extent broken in 1929 when Lord Hewart, then Lord Chief Justice of England, published "The New Despotism". In this, he declared:-

> "It is manifestly easy to point to a superficial contrast between what was done or attempted in the days of our least wise kings, and what is being done or attempted today. In those days the method was to defy Parliament, and it failed. In these days the method is to cajole, to coerce and to use Parliament, and it is strangely successful. The old despotism which was defeated offered Parliament a challenge. The new despotism, which is not yet defeated, gives Parliament an anaesthetic. The strategy is different but the goal is the same. It is to subordinate Parliament to evade the courts and to render the will or the caprice of the executive unfettered and supreme."

(Page 17)

Both on account of the high legal position of the author and the very detailed and technical competency with which he presented his theme made "The New Despotism" the most serious challenge which our modern political system has had to face. The situation was met by the appointment of a Committee of Ministers' Powers on terms of reference, which for the first time gave official recognition to the doctrine of Parliamentary sovereignty as a principle of the Constitution. This had to be firmly established beyond any question. "The New Despotism" was essentially a challenge to the concept of Parliamentary Sovereignty on which our modern political system rests. It is, therefore, not strange that the very doctrine which resulted in the conditions described in "The New Despotism" should be the basis on which the committee was to act. This doctrine of Parliamentary sovereignty rests only on the authority of one man, A. V. Dicey. As Professor Wade, in his introduction to the tenth edition of Dicey's "Law of the Constitution" points out:-

> "It can be the experience of few writers to find in the terms of reference to a Royal Commission or important departmental committee a direction that the enquiry should be into the very principles which the writer had propounded. Yet it was in 1929 within a few years

of Dicey's death that the Lord Chancellor of the day required the committee on Ministers' Powers what safeguards were desirable or necessary to secure the constitutional principles of the sovereignty of Parliament and the supremacy of the Law. The report of the Committee (Cmd 4060 1932) showed that the authority of "The Law and the Constitution" was accepted fifty years after its first appearance."

(Page XXI)

We may well ponder on our constitutional position in which the authority of a professor at Oxford can be evoked to upset a thousand years of unchallenged constitutional principles and to be relied upon to defeat the considered conclusion, based upon practical knowledge and experience of a Lord Chief Justice of England. The position is all the more remarkable in that Dicey himself, before he died, expressed the deepest sense of disillusionment at the constitutional developments under the very doctrine of Parliamentary sovereignty he had propounded.

Nine years before "The New Despotism" was published, Dicey was associated with Robert Rait as co-author in the work "Thoughts on the Scottish Union." In this, the authors compare the condition of our modern Parliament with that of the Scottish Parliament in the period following the reception of the Roman Civil Law in which they say:-

"Englishmen of today are not in a position to blame with severity the ease with which, in early times, the parliamentarians of Scotland allowed the legislative power of Parliament to slip into the hands of a Parliamentary committee. Our modern Cabinet perform most of the functions discharged by the Lords of the Articles. The Cabinet determines in effect what are the Bills, which shall be brought before Parliament. The Cabinet if it is a strong government, decides which of these Bills shall pass into law. The House of Commons still indeed tolerates debate but the Cabinet can put an end by various forms of closure...The Cabinet, it will be objected, is more or less though in a very indirect way, appointed by Parliament and the Lords of the Articles were under the Stuarts practically appointed by the King. Does there live any prophet bold enough to predict that the Cabinet itself may not some day come to be appointed, in fact, by managers or bosses who have got a firm hold of the party machine?"

(Page 39)

In the face of the growing totalitarian challenge which was to lead to the Second World to save democracy, real constitutional issues could not be freely examined. Any criticism of the principles of the Party Cabinet system could be denounced as being inspired by fascist and totalitarian sympathies. Despite, however, the fact that the Party Cabinet system had established itself as the champion of free democracy in the face of the totalitarian challenge, deep and searching doubts as to its implications were expressed by some responsible constitutional authorities.

In the middle of the war against Nazi Germany, Sir Carlton Allen, in his searching analysis of English Constitutional development under the title of "Law and Orders," remarks:-

"It is not, as some suppose, an overweening executive which establishes despotism; it is the philosophy of despotism which forges executive power into a weapon for the attainment of its ends."

(Page 292)

And he hopes that his work might be:-

"A warning against the threat of totalitarian tyranny from whatever quarter it may arise."

(Page 294)

In 1950 in the House of Lords, the late Viscount Chelwood drew attention to the position of the Cabinet by moving a resolution that:-

"The growing power of the Cabinet is a danger to the democratic constitution of the country."

He wound up the debate by saying:-

> "There is no doubt it is established, indeed no question
> can be raised against it...that the powers of the Cabinet
> are dictatorial. It is not a question of whether they
> are amenable to public opinion in the sense that is
> represented on the Cabinet...the people of the Kremlin
> would no doubt say the same thing about their decisions.
> The point is that there is no appeal against decisions of
> the Cabinet in executive matters. They decide whatever
> they like, whether for good reasons or for bad reasons...
> there is no appeal."

(H. of Lords (Hansard) 17th May, 1950. Cols. 327 & 377)

Writing under the significant title of "The Passing of Parliament," Professor Keeton in 1952 declared:-

> "Today in Great Britain we live on the edge of
> dictatorship. Transition would be easy, swift and it
> could be accomplished with complete legality. Already
> so many steps have been taken in this direction due
> to the completeness of the power possessed by the
> Government of the day and the absence of any real
> checks such as the terms of a written constitution or
> the existence of any effective second chamber that
> those still to be taken are small in comparison."

(Page 33)

Our system of government today is an illegality and a usurpation of legal constituted authority, made possible by the stranglehold which the modern party system has established over the membership of the House of Commons and sanctified by its doctrine of Parliamentary sovereignty.

THE ENGLISH PARLIAMENTARY CONSTITUTION

Nothing of the great and historic Parliamentary Constitution of England survives except for its meaningless forms, institutions, and ceremonies.

As Lord Justice Denning pointed out in his collection of essays under the title of "The Changing Law":-

> "Over one hundred years ago Parliament was no doubt, the supreme power in the land both in law and in fact... In practice sovereignty no longer rests in Parliament. It rests with the Executive...Once elected the leaders of the party are the sovereign power in the land."

The English Parliamentary constitution was, through all the centuries of its development the pride and glory of the English people. The constitution provided the mechanism of the most stable, strong and resilient system of free government derived solely from the consent of the people, themselves, by which they controlled their own destiny and welfare.

Five hundred years ago, Lord Justice Fortescue, Chancellor to Henry VI, writing while in exile after the defeat of his king in the Wars of the Roses, declared in "The Governance of England":-

> "But Blessyd be God, this land is ruled under a bettir lawe; and therefore the people thereof be not in such pernurie, nor thereby hurt in their persons, but thai bith welthe, and have all things necessarie to the sustenance of nature. Wherefore thae ben mighty and able to resiste the adversaries of this reaume, and to beete other reaumes that do or wolde do them wrong.

Lo this is the fruyt of Jus Polliticum et Regale under which we live."

(Edited by Plumber, Oxford, 1885, p. 115)

Edmund Burke, speaking three hundred years later, was able to say:-

"Our constitution is like our island which uses and restrains its subject sea; in vain the waves roar. In that Constitution I know and exultantly feel, both that I am free and I am not free dangerously to myself or to others. I know that no power on earth, acting as I ought to do, can touch my life, my liberty or my property. I have that inward and dignified consciousness of my own security and independence which constitutes and is the only thing that does constitute the proud and comfortable sentiment of freedom in the human breast. I know that if I possessed all the talents of the gentlemen on the side of the House I sit and on the other, I cannot by royal favour, or by popular delusion or by oligarchical cabal, elevate myself above a certain very limited point so as to endanger my own fall or the ruin of my country. I know there is an order that keeps things fast in their place; it is made to us and we are made to it."

(Speech House of Commons, 7th May, 1782)

Hallam, writing in 1818, could say:-

"No unbiased observer who derives pleasure from the welfare of his species, can fail to consider the long and uninterruptedly increasing prosperity of England as the most beautiful phenomenon in the history of mankind. Climates more propitious may impart more largely the mere enjoyments of existence, but in no other region have the benefits that political institutions can confer, been diffused over so extended a population, nor have any people so well reconciled the discordant elements of wealth, order and liberty. These advantages are surely not owing to the soil of the island nor to the latitude in which it is placed, but to the spirit of its laws, from which through various means the characteristic independence and industriousness of our nation have been derived. The Constitution of England, therefore must be to inquisitive men of all countries, far more to ourselves, an object of superior interest; distinguished, especially as it is from all free governments of powerful nations, which history has records by its manifesting, after the lapse of several centuries, not merely no symptom of irretrievable decay, but a more expansive energy."

(Europe in the Middle Ages, Chap. VIII, Part 1)

In 1905 Professor A. V. Dicey recorded that:-

"Faith in the English Constitution was fifty years ago the common characteristic of almost all our statesmen. This was a creed of no sudden growth. It had been preached by the genius of Burke, it was enforced by the arguments and learning of Hallam, it colours every page of Macaulay, it explains Wellington's celebrated declaration that the nature of man was incapable of creating by any effort, institutions of such paramount excellence as the Constitution which England enjoyed under the unreformed Parliament of 1830. The Whigs never desired to do more than to repair the revered fabric of our Constitution. Many of them held that the policy of reform was nothing but strengthening of the original foundations on which rested the institutions of England."

(Law and Public Opinion in England, 1905, p. 438)

The constitutional issues that now face us in England concern not only the British peoples but have a direct influence on the whole of western and a great part of eastern civilisation itself. This arises from the fact that there is not a single civilised nation in the world today which has not directly or indirectly drawn upon English constitutional example. The English conception of law and government has been so predominant that even in the turmoil of constitutional issues set up by the French Revolution the warning of Talleyrand can be heard:-

> "If the English Constitution is destroyed, the civilisation of the world will be shaken to its foundation."

(Duff Cooper Arrow Books, p. 142)

And a century later, it was the American historian, George Burton Adams, Emeritus Professor of History at Yale University, who declared:-

> "The unanimous judgement of the world at the beginning of the twentieth century is that the English Constitution is the best system of government yet devised...The English Constitution has made the circuit of the globe and become the common expression of civilised man...centuries of experiment unite to declare this the best result of all experience."

(The Origin of the English Constitution, p.1)

The English Parliamentary Constitution is the only surviving relic in the field of law and government of the practical realisation of medieval Christian ideals, which in the West aimed to fill the void created by the collapse of Roman imperialism. The Christian message was the emancipation of man and emphasised the divine quality of human destiny, based upon a society of justice and right as an approach to the kingdom of God upon earth.

In all the controversies generated by this search for a divine order, agreement existed on the fundamental principle of the absolute integrity of a Christian and this showed itself, not only in the opposition to slavery, but to any form of bondage of one Christian to another through social, political or economic circumstances beyond his control. Christ made man free, but as his freedom is conditional upon order, his freedom was bound by duties to maintain this order. Free Christian society was therefore a matter of legal relationships in which fundamental rights were balanced by equal counterbalancing duties. These rights and duties were established in law which no contract could alter. Thus parents had rights over their children but they also had duties which were the rights of the children. So had masters and servants rights and duties, so had landlords and tenants. The highest social relationship was the mutual rights and duties of ruler and subjects. Government authority was, therefore, a matter of which we now would call constitutional law as part of the general law of the whole community. As Otto Gierke in "Political Theories of the Middle Ages", as translated by F. W. Maitland, put it:-

> "The relationship between monarch and community was steadily conceived as a relationship which involved reciprocal rights and duties. Both monarch and community were 'subjects' of political rights and duties, and it was only the union of the two that the organic whole consisted. Moreover, in the community all the individuals stood in legal relationships to the monarch, relationships which properly deserved to be called legal and which were of a bilateral kind. Lordship, therefore, was never mere right; primarily it was duty; it was divine, but for that reason all the more onerous calling; it was a public office, a service rendered to the whole body. Rulers are instituted for the sake of peoples, not peoples for the sake of rulers. Therefore the power of the ruler is not absolute but limited by appointed bounds. His task is to further the common weal, peace and justice, the utmost freedom for all. In every breach of these duties and every transgression of the bounds that they set, legitimate lordship degenerates into tyranny. Therefore the doctrine of unconditioned duty of obedience was wholly foreign to the Middle Age. Far rather every duty of obedience was conditioned by the rightfulness of the command. That every individual must obey God rather than any earthly superior appeared as an absolutely indispensable truth...For one thing, it taught that every command which exceeded the limits of the ruler's authority was for his subjects a mere nullity and obliged none to obedience. And then again it proclaimed the right of resistance, and even armed resistance against compulsory enforcement of any unrighteous and tyrannical measure, such enforcement being regarded as an act of bare violence."

(Page 34)

The guiding principles of medieval law as it emerged from its pagan background was expressed by Hooker when he wrote:-

> "Of Law there can be no less acknowledged that her seat is the bosom of God, her voice the harmony of the world, the very least as feeling her care and the greatest not exempted from her power. Both angels and men and creatures, of what condition soever they be, though each in a different manner and yet with all uniform consent, admiring her as the mother of their peace and joy."

> (Of the Laws of Ecclesiastical Policy, Richard Hooker, Book 1, Ch. XVI-8, Oxford 1850, p. 34)

In the medieval age, Law, both as equity and utility, rested on the consent of those subject to it and, for its progressive development, was amenable to reason commanding such consent. Law enforcement was the first duty of the ruler, but he himself had to be held subject to the law, which he was sworn to obey but which he could neither change nor disregard. Law was thus a control on power on behalf of the people. To make such control effective required legal institutions by which law could be established outside the ruler's will and could be enforced against the ruler. Throughout the western communities, these legal institutions -the early forms of what we would now call parliamentary; were established and were being developed. As Hallam, in his "Europe during the Middle Ages" points out :-

> "Arbitrary rule, at least in theory, was uncongenial to the character of the northern nations. Neither the power of making laws nor that of applying them to the circumstances of particular cases, were left to the discretion of the Sovereign. The Lombard kings held assemblies every year at Pavia where the chief officers of the Crown and proprietors of lands deliberated on all legislative measures in the presence and nominally at least with the consent of the multitude. Frequent mention is made of similar public meetings in France by the historians of the Merowingian Kings and still more unequivocally by their statutes. These assemblies

have been called parliaments of the Champ de Mars...It is continually expressed in Charlemagne's capitularies and those of his family that they were enacted by general consent. In one of Louis the Debonair we trace the first germ of representative legislation... Fifty years after Charlemagne, his grandson Charles the Bald, succinctly expresses the theory of legislative power. 'A law' he says is made by the people's consent and the King's enactment."

(Ch. II, Sec. IV, 4th edit., p. 112)

In England, this medieval concept of law and government was threatened by the Norman conquest, and the native English reacted to it in the reign of William the Conqueror himself.

According to Hale's "History of the Common Law of England": -

"the English had a suspicion that they should suddenly have a change in their laws before they were aware of it. But it fell out much better. For first there arising some danger of a defection of the English, countenanced by the Archbishop of York, in the north, and Frederick Abbot of St. Albans in the south, the King, by the persuasion of Lancfranc, Archbishop of Canterbury, - 'pro bono pacis apud Berkamsted juravit super animam relinquias sancti Albani tactisque sacrosanctis evangeliis (ministrante juramento Abbate Frederico) et bonos et approbatas antiquas regni leges quas et pii Anglia reges ejus antecessores, et Maxime Rege Evardus Statuit inviolabiliter observeret : et sic pacificati ad propia laeti recessarunt' (Vide Mat. Paris in vita Frederica Abbatis sancti Albani.) But although now upon this capitulation, the ancient English laws were confirmed and namely the laws of St. Edward the Confessor, yet it appeared not what those laws were; and therefore..."

From this principle recognised by William the Conqueror, English law and government has never departed. The failure of William's successors to keep their oaths to uphold and administer only the established law of the land as recorded in various charters brought the Normans and the native English together and led to the momentous event in the fields of Runnymede in 1215 in the reign of King John. There was then produced that great record of English law known as Magna Carta, which aimed to establish the fundamental principles of English law applicable at that time.

Magna Carta, known also as the Great Charter of English liberties is the fundamental and constituent instrument of English government and established the principle that the only basis of authority of the united Anglo-Norman nation was the law of the land derived solely from the consent of the people to which every ruler of England had to adhere and which he would be compelled to observe. The instrument of observance by rulers and subjects alike was the High and Most Honourable Court of Parliament instituted by Magna Carta for this purpose as the supreme authority of the English nation.

As Blackstone put it:-

> "The main constitution of Parliament, as it now stands, was marked as long ago as the seventeenth year of King John A.D. 1215 in the great charter granted by that prince wherein he promised to summon all Archbishops, Bishops, Abbots, Earls and Greater Barons personally and all other tenants in chief under the Crown by the Sherriff and Bailiffs to meet at a certain place within forty days notice to assess aids and scutages when necessary."

Magna Carta is, therefore, the constituent law of the English Parliamentary Constitution and English Law derived solely from the consent of the people, for as Burke pointed out:-

> "In all forms of government the people is the true legislator, and whether the immediate and instrumental cause of the law be a single person or many, the remote and efficient cause is the consent of the people either actually or implied, and such consent is absolutely vital to its validity."

To give practical effect to this concept of law, it has been established that English law is the product of reason commanding or likely to command the consent of the people, and as no one has the right to change the law merely on the ground of personal reason, its development and application must be governed by precedent of already established law and must be directed to fundamental ends already consented to in particular to the terms of Magna Carta and subsequently re-interpretations in the form of parliamentary enactments.

The application and interpretation of English Law is therefore not determined by a single source and is always the final product of advice and consent. In English courts of law, the judges do not establish the law, but they produce the evidence of law in their reasoned judgements, which, if unchallenged on appeal or in Parliament, is accepted as law.

A legally constituted Parliament is the guarantee of the absolute integrity of every individual person with his rights and his duties which those rights impose to lead the life he wishes free from social, political and economic coercion or exploitation and is therefore opposed to every form of arbitrary power exercised by any man or group of men over their fellow men by any legal, political or economic theory.

This Edmund Burke emphasised in his speech in Westminster Hall on 16th February 1788, when he declared:-

> "The King has no arbitrary power, the House of Lords have not nor the Commons nor the whole legislature... No man can lawfully govern himself according to his own will, much less can one person be governed by the will of another...Arbitrary power is not to be had by conquest, nor can any sovereign have it by succession, for no man can succeed to fraud, rapine and violence; neither by compact, covenant or submission - for men cannot covenant themselves out of their rights or their duties; not by any other means can arbitrary power be conveyed to any man. Those who give to other such rights, perform acts that are void as they are given, good and valid only as tending to subject themselves and those who act with them to the divine displeasure because morally there can be no such power. Those who give and those who receive arbitrary power are alike

criminal; and there is no man but is bound to resist it to the best of his power, wherever it shall show its face to the world. It is a crime to bear it, when it can be rationally shaken off. Nothing but absolute impotence can justify men not resisting it to the utmost of their ability. Law and arbitrary power are in eternal enmity."

English law and government was already well consolidated when at the close of the Middle Ages, a completely opposite concept of law and government was by the Renaissance introduced in the Western world.

The Renaissance led to a revival of the study of Roman Law and, as a result of academic activity, displaced to a large extent, the native laws based upon medieval conceptions. It is easy enough to understand how Roman law made its great appeal. To an age searching for legal stability, the discovery of a ready-made legal code based upon the long and rich experience of Roman civilisation would appear as a godsend. Its reception avoided the long and tedious process in the development of principles derived from native law and custom, which only in England had approached the stage of a Common Law for the whole community.

There was, however, one fatal defect in the Roman jurisprudence as revived in the Renaissance. Whereas the law of the Roman people was the product of the juristic process, based upon the fundamental concept that the legal authority was derived from the citizen's consent and formulated first in the Laws of the Twelve Tables, the Roman law of the Renaissance was the codified Roman Law of the Eastern Empire after the fall of Rome and had, therefore, no basis in the consent of the people, and instead its authority rested on the despotic will of the Eastern emperors. This Roman Civil code specifically rejected the authority of the people on the ground that they had unconditionally surrendered their power into the hands of their rulers. It is on this principle that the modern revived Roman Civil law is based and is expressed in the Institutes of Justinian in the following terms:

"That which seems good to the Emperor has also the force of law; for the people by the Lex Regia which is passed to confer on him his powers, made over to him their whole power and authority. Therefore whatever the Emperor ordains by rescript or decides in adjudging a cause or lays down by edict, is unquestionably law."

(Trans. T. C. Sanders, Liber. I, Tit. II, Sect. 6, Longmans 1900, p. 10)

This doctrine of the Lex Regia was, in fact, the only fundamental principle of law which the reception of the Roman Code introduced. As Otto Gierke, in his "Political Theories of the Middle Ages" remarks:-

"Ever since the days of the Glossators (the twelfth century) the universally accepted doctrine was that an act of alienation performed by the people in the Lex Regia was for positive law the basis of the modern as well as the ancient empire. For this cause it was all the easier to generalise this truth concerning the highest of all temporal communities until it appeared as a principle grounded in divine and natural law. Indeed, that the legal title to all rulership lies in voluntary and contractual submission to the rulers could therefore be propounded as a philosophic axiom."

(Page 39)

The effect of this was that the ruler was not subject to law as he, as author of all law, was above it. As Gierke further remarked:-

"...The Doctrine of the absolute subjection of positive law (jus civile) to the sovereign power...which worked a revolution in the world of archaic German ideas, taught that the jus civile was the freely created product of the power of the community, an instrument mutable in accordance with the estimates of utility, a set of rules that had no force of their own. It followed that in every community the wielder of sovereignty stood above the positive law that prevailed therein. Nay, always more decisively, men found the distinguishing note of sovereignty, ecclesiastical and temporal, in the fact the sovereign was not bound by any human law. The advocates of Ruler's sovereignty identified positive law with the expressing or tacitly declared will of the Ruler. They placed the Ruler before and above the statutes made by him or his predecessors. They taught that he for his part was not bound by the statute, but might in every single case apply or break it as need might be. Even from the twelfth century onwards, jurisprudence laid stress on those Roman texts that made for this result."

(The Political Theories of the Middle Age, Trans. F. W. Maitland, pp. 76-77)

Whatever great technical qualities the Roman Civil code preserved from its Roman origin, its revival devastated and demoralised the Christian foundation of Western civilisation by undermining the basic social principle of mutual rights and duties. The result of the reception of Roman Civil code was to vest the powerful with legal rights and no duties while the weaker were loaded with duties and no rights. The honourable condition of liberty based upon service was converted into a condition of virtual servitude. Thus wherever and whenever Roman law was received, we see the forlorn struggle of the people to preserve their ancient rights and the bitter peasant revolts in the different communities.

The reception of the Roman Civil code completely reversed the direction of medieval constitutional development. Instead of aiming to control the arbitrary will of the ruler, the new constitutional system had the sole purpose of making his arbitrary will effective. The rule of law by which all government is justified thus underwent a complete inversion of meaning, for what had been the basis of law in the medieval sense was now the beginning of lawlessness in the Roman sense and every attempt to assert ancient rights was now sedition. The latter Middle Age is thus a period of confusion and contradiction.

Professor McIlwain of Harvard gives us a general description of this confusion in "The Growth of Political Thought in the West." when he wrote:-

"If one were attempting to apply the word 'medieval' to anything reactionary, as thoughtless people usually do today, it might be well to ponder that...political absolutism is an achievement of modern times. The Middle Ages would have none of it. But with medieval monarchy as with feudal relations, the prevailing theory was one thing, the actual facts were another. A nobler conception of kingship - a higher conception of government even - has seldom been expressed than that of the Middle Ages. Yet injustice was rife and private war almost constant, the lords and kings alike often acted arbitrarily and oppressively. The main political defect of the time was not lack of principles but an almost total absence of any effective sanction for them, and this is undoubtedly one of the chief reasons for the later acquiescence in royal absolutism."

(P.197)

But in fact, there is another explanation. The confusion arose by making arbitrary power a legal force by the reception of the Roman Civil code. J. H. Figgis, in "The studies of Thought from Gerson to Grotius," declared:-

"The Civil Law was triumphant. The conditions of a full theory of sovereignty existed and were active. There was a very real danger that this discovery - for it was a discovery - of a power that could not be bound by law because it could make law would produce a more enduring tyranny than any hitherto known and it did do this in some places, especially as in most states it was no assembly or republic to whose advantage this boon had come."

(2nd Edit., 1907, Cambridge U. P. 1908, p. 101)

Paul Vinogradoff pointed out in "Roman Law in Medieval Europe":-

"It is evident, to begin with, that the reception of Roman law depended largely on political causes. This legal system was subordinate to the idea of the State towering over individuals or classes and free from the intermixture of private and public interests characteristics of feudalism. It was bound to appeal to the minds of all pioneers of the State conception -

to ambitious emperors, grasping territorial princes, reforming legists and even clerical representatives of law and order."

(P. 130)

Even the legal development of English liberty was not unaffected by Roman legal indoctrination. In the same work Paul Vinogradoff remarks:-

"The historical growth of English villeinage did not necessarily involve its treatment on the basis of serfdom or slavery. But the infusion of Roman doctrine made the legal treatment of villeinage harder than might have been the case otherwise, while the partial reservations introduced by the emperors and admitted by Bracton did not carry much weight in practice."

(Ibid)

Thus, Roman law was introduced into the medieval world with those tenets which legalised the abuse and corruption of power, which is to this day one of the greatest evils of the modern western world. Professor G. W. Keeton, in "The Elementary Principles of Jurisprudence," points out:-

"It has often been remarked that the chief effect of the renaissance in political organisation and in legal thought was to destroy all limitations on the activities of the rulers in relation to their subjects, leaving the latter face to face with the uncontrolled authority of the sovereign. Regarded from that point of view, modern totalitarianism is merely the culminating point of a long historical process which connects the Renaissance despots with Hitler and Mussolini."

(2nd edit., 1949, Pitmans, p. 60)

The reception of the Roman Civil Law completely destroyed the basis of medieval parliamentary institutions as representatives of the community, though the institutions themselves frequently were retained to provide an accepted and recognised legal form for the new innovation. How this worked out in a single community can be seen in the constitutional developments in Scotland following the reception of Roman Law.

According to A.R.G. McMillan in his work "Evolution of the Scottish Judiciary," Scotland had for centuries been a common law country with medieval conceptions and institutions not unlike those of England. As McMillan points out, the king was the fountain of justice and the administrative head of state, but he was not the source of law which was to be found in the usages and customs of the people as declared by their representatives in Parliament. (Edinburgh, 1941, IX)

In 1370 the Scottish Parliament, under strong Civil Law influence, virtually abdicated its power to an independent committee which finally became the College of Justice. It was by this committee that the Civil Law was introduced into Scotland, though never empowered to do so by a Scottish Parliament.

In "The Institutions of the Law in Scotland," by Sir George MacKenzie, written in the time of Charles II, we read:-

> "The Civil Law is much respected generally so it has great influence in Scotland except where their own express laws or customs have receded from it. And by the Common Law in our Acts of Parliament is meant the Civil Law of the Romans."

The constitutional consequences of the reception of Roman Law can be seen when MacKenzie writes in Book 1 Title II:-

> "The King is the author and fountain of all power and is an absolute Prince having as much power as any King or potentate whatsoever, deriving his power from God Almighty and so not from the people...The legislative power is only in the King and the estates of Parliament only consent and in Parliament the King has a negative voice whereby he may not only hinder any Act to pass but even any overture to be first debated there."

In Roman Civil Law theory, the power of the King was absolute, and the only check on his will was his conscience, for which he was answerable only to God. Beyond this, there was nothing to prevent the authority of the King being exercised in his name and in consequence, there arose the greatest of all evils, the control of national affairs by favourites and courtiers or even worse, when the King was weak, by ambitious and envious subjects, organised in factions who sought the King's authority for their own ends. Such an abuse and corruption of Government had no legal remedy under the Civil Law, and by the corruption of the Parliamentary institutions it could be given a legal and constitutional form. This is a development which arose in almost all communities where on the reception of the Civil Law, medieval Parliamentary institutions were retained. It can be seen in the constitutional development, or rather decay, in Scotland. Robert Rait dealing with the period from 1406 to 1560 in "The Scottish Parliament before the Union of the Crowns" describes this corruption of the Scottish Parliament when he writes :-

> "Each of the ever changing factions who strove for political importance has an object in availing themselves of the advantages of Parliamentary and legal sanction. The delegation of work to committees made it certain that the party could absolutely rely on having its way and the form of law was desirable as legalising their present action and as forming some kind of defence should misfortune overtake them. Similarly the King, when he chanced to be powerful, found in his Parliament a most useful instrument for carrying out his wishes. It was for ruling faction and for powerful King alike the best method of registering and declaring the will or policy of the rulers of Scotland for the time being. A Parliament, and just this kind of Parliament, was always wanted by the government."

(Page 9)

The historic unity and development of the English Parliamentary constitution lies in its total rejection and resistance to the despotic and arbitrary tenets which the reception of Roman Civil law was establishing in the western world.

Thus, when all the other communities of the West lost their medieval institutions and social principles that went with them, in England, they were developed and strengthened and remain to this day as the basis of constitutional institutions. As Professor G.M. Trevelyan, O.M. in his introduction to Professor Anthony Steel's "Richard II" remarks:-

> "...medieval institutions will not have disappeared from
> our land unless and until some authoritarian system
> succeeds in abolishing our Parliament, our universities,
> our churches and our Common Law."

(Page VII)

This is not to say that English Law has not drawn heavily on Roman jurisprudence, but, like the Latin words in the English language, Roman legal ideas have been incorporated into English law without affecting its basic character as the law of the English People. But through the centuries, the struggle against Roman Civil Law indoctrination continued unceasingly in England, for never at any time have the people of England abandoned the conception of law as springing from their own consent.

The symbol of the vast struggle against the legal acceptance of despotic and arbitrary power was Magna Carta.

The principle that Magna Carta established was the government of England is subject to English Law which the government could not change or disregard.

Though Magna Carta makes no direct reference to the doctrines of the Civil Law, it nevertheless emphasises the Lex terrae, which Seldon in his "Ad Fletam Dissertatio" (Ionnis Seldeni, David Ogg, Cambridge U. P. 1925, p. 173) claims to be in opposition to Lex Regia of the revived Roman Law. That this must have been the spirit of the times is borne out seventeen years later in the declaration in the Provisions of Merton of 1233 which still stands first in our Statute Book, in the rejection of a Civil Law proposal:-

> "Nolumus leges Anglae mutare", which in the authorised
> translation reads, "They would not change the laws of
> the realm which hitherto have been used and approved."

In the same century, we have the work of Bracton, the earliest commentator on English law who though a student and admirer of Roman law, nevertheless rejected the tenet of the Lex Regia by his formula, which has ever since been the touchstone of English constitutional government:-

> "The King himself ought not to be the subject to man but subject to God and the law, for the law makes the king. Let the king then attribute to the law what the law attributes to him, namely dominion and power, for there is no king where the will and not the law has domination."
>
> (Laws of England, Halsbury 2nd edit., Vol. 16, note n, p. 382)

In the 14th century, in the reign of Richard II, we have the Parliamentary declaration:-

> "The realm of England hath never been unto this hour neither by consent of our Lord the King and the Lords of Parliament shall it ever be ruled or governed by the Civil Law."

This was finally vindicated in the revolution of 1399 when Richard was deposed, and Henry IV enthroned on his declaration that he would rule not by his will but solely by advice of his councillors.

There is the recognition of the principle by Lord Justice Fortescue in the 15th century in the period of the Wars of the Roses when he himself was an exile with the Queen and the Prince of Wales in France where the Roman Code had been received and its consequences could be observed. In his "De Laudibus Legem Angliae," Fortescue wrote:-

> "For the King of England is not able to change the laws of his kingdom at his pleasure, for he rules his people with a power not only regal but also political. If his power over them were only regal then he might change the laws of his realm and charge his subjects with taxes and other burdens without their consent: and such is the dominion that the Civil Laws claim when they state: 'The Prince's pleasure has the force of law'. But the case is far otherwise with a King ruling his people politically; he neither can change the law without the consent of his subjects nor yet charge them with impositions against their will. Wherefore his people fairly and freely enjoy

and occupy their own goods being ruled by such laws that they themselves desire."

(Trans. S.B. Chrimes, Cambridge U. P. 1942, p. 25)

Professor Haseltine pointed out in his general preface to Chrimes' "Sir John Fortescue":-

> "On the continent during the age of the Renaissance, the law books of the Post Glossatorial or Bartolist Civilians were a most potent factor in the development of the constitutional and legal institutions along romantic lines. In Tudor England, on the other hand, it was the literature written by lawyers, trained in the history, principles and methods of the Common Law which proved to be one of the most influential of all dominant factors making for a further development of the constitutional and legal institutions inherited from the Middle Ages along the lines of a policy that one and the same time was conservative, reformative and constructive...Suffusing the literature of the law, this spirit was transmitted to the Statesmen who saved England from the absolutism on the continent which had been so largely founded on Roman ideas of law and government."

> (De Laudibus Legum Anglia Fortescue Trans. S. B. Chrimes, Cambridge U. P. 1942, General Preface, p. XXXI)

Whilst the Kings of other nations flaunted their sovereignty above all law, the kings of England gloried in their Parliamentary position. Henry VIII, one of the most arrogant of all English kings, declared that:-

> "We be informed by our judges that we at no time stand so highly in our estate royal as in the time of Parliament, wherein we as head and you as members are conjoined and knit together into one body politic, so as whatsoever offence or injury during that time is offered to the meanest members of the House is judged as done against our person and the whole court of

Parliament, which prerogative is so great...as all acts and processes coming out of any of the inferior courts for the time cease and give place to the highest."

(Hatsell Precedents, Vol. 1 Page 57)

In this reign we have the declaration of Parliamentary supremacy (25 Henry VIII c. 21.):-

"...This realm recognising no superiority under God... hath been and is free from subjection to any man's laws but only to such as have been devised, made and obtained within this realm for the Wealth of the same... the people of this your Realm have taken at their free liberty, by their own consent to be used among them and have bound themselves by long use and custom to the observance of the same... It standeth therefore with natural equity and good reason that in all and every such laws human made within this realm... Your majesty and your Lords Spiritual and Temporal and Commons, representing the whole state of your Realm in this your Most High Court of Parliament have full power and authority not only to dispense with those and all other human laws of this your realm...to abrogate annul, amplify or diminish as it shall be seem, unto your Majesty and the Nobles and Commons in your Parliament, meet and convenient for the wealth of your realm."

(The Statutes Revised, 2nd edit., Vol. 1, 1533, p. 294)

The legal supremacy of Parliament is, therefore, the symbol of the total rejection and repudiation by the English people of any doctrine of surrendered power and has stood through the centuries as the assurance guaranteed by Magna Carta that never, in fact or fiction, conditionally or unconditionally, by conquest or by grant have the English people surrendered their power, their rights and liberties into the hands of their rulers or anyone else.

The great charter of English Liberties under its name of Magna Carta is, therefore, the constituent law of the English Parliamentary constitution, and it is from the fundamental law established by Magna Carta that Parliament derives its legal supremacy and authority. It has thus been recognised through the centuries.

Coke, one of our greatest of Common Law lawyers, has this to say of Magna Carta:-

> "Though it be in forme charter, yet granted by assent and authorities of Parliament, Littleton here sayeth it is a statute. The Parliamentary charter hath divers appelation in law. Here it is called Magna Carta, not for the length or largeness of it...but in respect of the great weightiness and weightie greatness of the matter contained in few words, being the fountaine of all the fundamental laws of the realm and therefore it may be truly said of it that it is a magnum in parvo...This statute of Magna Carta hath been confirmed thirty times and commanded to be put into execution. By the statute 25, Edward I, judgement given against any part of the Charters of Magna Carta or Charter de Foresta, are adjudged void. And by Statute of 42, Edward III C. I. If any statute be made against either of these charters it shall be void"

(1st Inst., 18th edit., Sec. 108, 81a)

The fundamental character of Magna Carta has perhaps been best described by Taswell-Langmead in his "English Constitutional History" when he writes:-

> "Three great political documents, in the nature of fundamental compacts between the Crown and the Nation, stand out as prominent landmarks in English Constitutional history. Magna Carta, the Petition of Right, and the Bill of Rights constitute in the words of Lord Chatham, 'The Bible of the English Constitution'. In each of these documents, whether it be of the thirteenth or the seventeenth century, is observable the common characteristic of professing to introduce nothing new. Each professed to assert rights and liberties which were

already old, and sought to redress grievances which were for the most part themselves innovations upon the ancient liberties of the people...The importance of Magna Carta can hardly be exaggerated. It has been characterised by Hallam as 'the keystone of English liberty'to which all that has been since added is 'little or more than confirmation or commentary' and Sir James Mackintosh has insisted upon the noticeable fact that the consequences of its principles were but slowly and gradually evolved as circumstances required, during the five succeeding centuries."

(8th edit., 1919, Ch. 4, p. 95)

E. J. Creasy, in his "Rise and Progress of the English Constitution" has this to say, in regard to Magna Carta:-

"In Magna Carta itself, that is to say, in a solemn instrument deliberately agreed on by the King, the prelates, the great barons, the gentry and the burghers, the yeomanry, and all the freedom of the realm, at an epoch which we have the right to consider the commencement of our nationality, and in the statute entitled 'Confirmatio Cartarum' which is to be read as a supplement to Magna Carta, we can trace these great principles in germ, and some more fully revealed. And thus at the very dawn of the history of the present English nation, we behold the foundations of our great political institutions imperishably laid. These great primeval and enduring principles of our constitution are as follows:- The government of the country by a hereditary sovereign, ruling with limited powers, and bound to consult Parliament comprising hereditary peers and elective representatives of the Commons, That the subject's money shall not be taken by the sovereign unless with the subject's consent, expressed by his representative in Parliament. That no man be arbitrarily fined or imprisoned or in any way punished except by a lawful trial. Trial by Jury. That justice may not be sold or delayed. These great constitutional principles can all be proved either by express terms, or by fair implication from Magna Carta and its above mentioned supplement."

(pp. 3&4)

In a note in the 1932 edition of Halsbury's "Laws of England," we are told that:-

"Magna Carta is still in force and binding upon the Crown so far as its provisions are not out of date or repealed."

After a reference to the petition of Right, this note concludes with the statement that:-

"These statutes must not be regarded as curtailment of existing prerogatives but as fundamental laws of England."

(3rd edit., Vol. 6, Note m, p. 450)

Magna Carta remains the outstanding symbol of English legal nationality and like the symbol of the Cross to Christendom, so this charter rallied and sustained the English people in their greatest aspiration in their noble and civilising achievement. As the poet Southey put it:-

"That charter that should make thee morn and night,
Be thankful for thy birthright, Englishman.
That holy Charter that shouldst thou permit
Force to destroy or fraud to undermine
Thy children's groans will persecute thy soul
For they must bear the burden of thy crime."

(Epitaph of King John, Morning Post, 28th May, 1798)

Except for the paltry and insincere attempt by Richard II to establish his kingship on the tenets of the Roman Civil Law, the principles of the English Parliamentary constitution had never been challenged in principle till the seventeenth century. It was then that the Scottish Kings born and bred in the doctrine of Roman Civil law kingship came to the Common

Law throne of England. To these Scottish kings, their conception of kingship appeared to them as a principle grounded in divine and natural law, as Otto Gierke put it in his "Political Theories of the Middle Age". The English Parliamentary constitution was to them a fundamental violation of kingship as they sincerely believed and they could not reconcile themselves to the acceptance of a position that their sovereignty was subject to the advice and consent of the other institutions of Parliament or that their Ministers should be responsible to anyone but themselves. It was from these Scottish kings that there arose the idea that there was an antagonism between king and Parliament which survives to this day.

In the mounting conflict between the conceptions of Roman kingship of the early Stuarts and the English Parliament, the issue of Roman sovereignty and fundamental law came to the fore. In the period from the accession of James I to the Act of Settlement almost a century later, there is one constant theme, namely the vindication of the fundamental or constitutional law of the English system of government. In that century, the great constitutional laws were enacted which still stand upon our Statute Book, be they Petition of Right, the Act for the Abolition of the Star Chamber, the Habeas Corpus Acts, the Bill of Rights or the Act of Settlement, they all refer explicitly or implicitly to Magna Carta, as fundamental to English law and government.

In the second act of the first Parliament of James I, we have a reference to the words "Fundamental Law." This act, passed at the desire of the new king, but which came to nothing, dealt with the appointment of commissioners to negotiate a political union between England and Scotland in its preamble established significantly as a matter of record that the new Scottish king:-

> "hath vouchsafed to express many ways how far it is
> and ever shall be from his royal and sincere care and
> affection to the subjects of England to alter or innovate
> the fundamental and ancient laws, privileges and good
> customs of this kingdom whereby not only his regal
> authority but the people's security...are preserved."

(Statutes at Large, Vol. 2 I, Jac. J.C. 2, 1603, p.337)

How disturbed the English were by the new conceptions which this Scottish king had brought with him is shown by the fact that James had to explain the difference between the Civil Law of Scotland and the Common Law of England. Speaking to the Houses of Parliament in 1607, James explained that:-

> "The meaning of the words "Fundamental Laws" you shall perceive more fully hereafter, when I handle the objection of the difference of laws, for they (the Scots) intend thereby only those laws whereby confusion is avoided and their king's descent maintained...not meaning as you do the Common Law; for they have none but that which is called the Lex Regia."
>
> (Parliamentary or Constitutional History of England, Vol. 5, p. 199)

Two years later, in 1609, James again had occasion to address the Houses of Parliament on the question of fundamental law. Dr. Cowell, a Civilian, had been propounding the Civil Law conception of Kingship to which Parliament had taken a strong and pronounced objection, especially when it appeared that in private, James had expressed approval of Dr. Cowell's thesis. James found it necessary to tell Parliament exactly where he stood. He had to do this by explaining that he was speaking as an Englishman.

> "showing this people that...as we lived in a settled state of a kingdom which was governed by its own fundamental laws and orders, that according thereunto they now being assembled for this purpose in Parliament to consider how to help such a king..."
>
> (Parliamentary or Constitutional History of England, Appendix p. 7)

In the reign of Charles I, the conflict over the constitutional implications of the Roman sovereignty of kings and the supremacy of the English Common Law reached a more bitter stage.

In 1627 the issue arose directly on the momentous debates in Parliament on the liberty of the subject which resulted in the enactment of The Petition of Right. An amendment was proposed that the king's sovereignty should be accepted. This amendment was rejected not only on behalf of the king but on behalf of Parliament. John Pym, the Parliamentary leader in the House of Commons, declared:-

> "All our petition is for the laws of England and this power (of sovereignty) seems to be another distinct power from the power of the law; I know how to add sovereign to his person but not to his power and we cannot leave to him a sovereign power; we also were never possessed of it."
>
> (Rushworth Vol. 1)

In the same debate, Coke himself took part and is reported to have said:-

> "Look into all the petition of former times, they never petition wherein there was a saving of the King's sovereignty. I know prerogative is a part of the law, but sovereign power is no parliamentary word. In my opinion it weakens Magna Carta and all our statutes; for they are absolute without any saving of sovereign power. And shall we now add it, we shall weaken the foundation of law and then the building must needs fall. Take we heed what we yield unto. Magna Carta is such a fellow that he will have no sovereign. I wonder this sovereign was not in Magna Carta or in confirmations of it; if we grant this amendment, by implication we give a sovereign power above all these laws. Power in law is taken for power with force."
>
> (Historical Collections, Rushworth, Vol. 1, p. 562)

In 1628, there were the proceedings against Dr. Mainwaring, student of the Civil Law, who had extolled the Civil Law rights of Kings. In this connection, the House of Commons issued a declaration which began:-

> "For a more effectual prevention of the apparent ruin and destruction of this kingdom which must necessarily ensue, if the good and fundamental laws and customs herein established be brought into contempt and violated and that form of government thereby altered

by which it hath so long been maintained in peace and happiness..."

(State Trials, Vol. 3, Col. 338)

In 1637 we had the Hampden Ship Money case on the right of taxation based entirely on Fundamental law. This was finally resolved by the judgement of the House of Lords:- "That the resolutions of the judges touching the Shipping Money and the judgement given against Mr. Hampden in the Exchequer and all proceedings thereon are against the Great Charter and therefore void in law."

The judges in this case were impeached by the House of Commons on the grounds that:-

> "Being one of the Justices of the said Court in the King's Bench, hath traitorously and wickedly endeavoured to subvert the fundamental laws and established government of the realm of England and instead thereby to introduce an arbitrary and tyrannical government against law which he hath declared by traitorous and wicked words, opinions, judgements, practices and actions."
>
> (State Trials, Vol. 4, Col. 11)

With the trial of Strafford, we have Lord Keeper Finch, Sir George Ratcliffe, Lord Kimbolton, Denzil Holles, Sir Arthur Haselrigg, John Pym, John Hampden, William Strode, Lord Strange, Archbishop Laud, all in one way or another accused of the crime of subverting the fundamental laws of England.

In the rising crisis of the constitution leading to the civil wars, the issue of fundamental law is ever present. In December, 1641, we have the Grand Remonstrance of the House of Commons, in which it was declared:-

> "The root of all this mischief we find to be a malignant and pernicious design of subverting the fundamental laws and principles of government upon which the religion and justice of this kingdom are firmly established."
>
> (Parliamentary History of England (Hansard) Vol. 2, Col. 946)

In 1646 we have the "Declaration of the Commons" assembled in Parliament of their true intention concerning the ancient and fundamental government of the kingdom and the government of the Church, the present peace securing the people against arbitrary government...In this declaration, issued in the middle of the civil wars, the House of Commons declared that:-

> "Wherein we are so far from altering the fundamental constitution and government of this kingdom by king, Lords and Commons, that we have only desired that with the consent of the King such powers..."

(Ibid. Vol. 3, Col. 458)

Then followed the Commonwealth period in which the appeal to fundamental law was even louder. We have the trials of John Lilburn and Dr. John Hewitt, and also those of William Penn and William Mead, all filled with reference and discussion of fundamental law. We have the political writings of William Prynne on "Fundamental Liberties of all English Freemen," as well as other legal tracts dealing with fundamental law.

The Restoration of 1660 was entirely based on fundamental law. In the letters which Charles II addressed to General Monk, to the Speaker of the House of Commons, to the House of Lords, and to the Lord Mayor and Aldermen of the City of London, each had a specific reference to fundamental law. In his declaration of Breda, Charles says:-

> "And to the end that fear of punishment may not engage any conscience to themselves of what is past to a perseverance in guilt for the future, opposing the quiet and happiness of the country in the restoration both of the king and peers and people to their just ancient fundamental rights, we do these present declare that we do grant a free and general pardon..."

(Parliamentary History of England (Hansard)Vol. 4, Col. 16)

At the actual restoration, both Houses of Parliament did:-

"Own and declare that (according to the ancient and fundamental laws of this kingdom) the government ought to be by King, Lords and Commons."

(Parliamentary History of England (Hansard) Vol. 4, Col. 25)

Finally, the event of the abdication of James II which led to the English Revolution of 1688, was associated with fundamental law. The English Convention Parliament which legalised the Revolution, declared:-

"That King James II having endeavoured to subvert the Constitution of the Kingdom by the advice of Jesuits and other wicked persons violated the fundamental laws and withdrawn himself out of the kingdom has abdicated the government and that the throne is thereby vacant."

(Ibid. Vol. 5, Col. 50)

The Revolution of 1688 restored the Parliamentary constitution on to its legal foundations by the Bill of Rights by, which it was enacted by authority of Parliament:-

"All and singular rights and liberties asserted and claimed in the said declaration are the true and indubitable rights and liberties of the people of this kingdom and so shall be esteemed allowed and judged deemed and taken to be and that all and every one of the particulars aforesaid shall be firmly and strictly holden and observed as they as they are expressed in the said declaration. And all officers and ministers whatsoever shall serve their majesties and their successors according to the same in all times to come."

(The Statutes Revised, 2nd. Edit., Vol. 1, p. 694)

The Bill of Rights, the nearest thing we have of a code of our Parliamentary Constitution, was confirmed as a fundamental law of

England. The Bill of Rights was followed by the Act of Settlement of 1701, which Hallam described as;-

> "The seal of our constitutional laws, the compliment of the Revolution itself and the Bill of Rights and the last great Statute which restrains the power of the Crown."

This Act concluded with its great peroration:-

> "And whereas the laws of England are the birthright of the people thereof and all the Kings and Queens who shall ascend the throne of this realm ought to administer the government of the same according to the said laws and all their officers and ministers ought to serve them respectively according to the same. The said Lords Spiritual and Temporal and Commons do therefore humbly pray that all the laws and statutes of this realm for securing the established religion and the rights and liberties of the people thereof and all other laws and statutes of the same now in force may be ratified and confirmed. And the same are by his Majesty by and with the advice and consent of the said Lords spiritual and temporal and commons and by the authority of the same ratified and confirmed accordingly."

By maintaining the absolute supremacy of Parliament, the English people maintained the supremacy of their own laws and defeated every corruption of political, economic and social power attempted by rulers or subjects alike, and preserved their national independence from foreign domination, whether military or economic.

The enduring strength and stability of the English Parliamentary constitution through all the centuries of its existence arose from the fact that it was founded in the law of the land derived from the consent of the people, which no one could alter or disregard and to which the king was sworn, and all his ministers were bound. This was the Rule of Law in England defined in classical form by Walter Paley in his "Moral and Political Philosophy" when he wrote:-

"By the constitution of a country is meant so much of its law as relates to the designation and form of the legislature; the rights and functions of several parts of the legislative body, the constitution, officers, offices and jurisdiction of the courts of justice. The constitution is one principle division, section or title of the code of public laws, distinguished from the rest only by the superior importance of the subject which it treats. Therefore the terms Constitutional and Unconstitutional mean legal and illegal. The distinction and ideas which these terms denote are founded in the same authority with the law of the land on any other subject; and is to be ascertained by the same enquiries. In England, the system of public jurisprudence is made up of Acts of Parliament, of decisions of courts of law and of immemorial usages. Consequently, these are the principles of which the English Constitution consists, the sources from which our knowledge of its nature and limitations is to be deduced, and the authorities to which all appeal ought to be made and by which every constitutional doubt and question can alone be decided..."

(12th edit., 1799, Vol. II, Ch. VII, p. 190)

Till the Reform Act of 1832, seditious conspiracy was always defined as "exciting hatred and contempt of the government and constitution of the realm as by law established."

In every edition of Dicey's "Law of the Constitution" from 1885 to 1969, the following words from the original lectures have been repeated:-

"The true law of the constitution is to be gathered from the sources whence we collect the law of England in respect to any other topic, and forms as interesting and as distinct, though not as well explored, a field of legal study or legal exposition as any which can be found. The subject is one which has not yet been fully mapped out. Teachers and pupils alike therefore suffer from the inconvenience as they enjoy the interest of exploring a province of law which has not yet been entirely reduced to order."

It is this obscurity of our great heritage of law and government in which our modern age has lost itself.

In England today, we are living under that very concept of law which the Roman Civil code introduced into the western world at the Renaissance and which, ever since, the English people have repudiated and rejected as totally lawless. Austinian jurisprudence under which the party cabinet has achieved arbitrary power marks the greatest legal convulsion in the whole history of the English people.

As Professor G. W. Keeton has pointed out in his "Elementary Principles of Jurisprudence":-

> "Although if legal thought in England is scrutinised somewhat narrowly, Austin's work may seem to make a fresh departure, in a very real sense, he may be regarded as continuing a line of development which began at the renaissance."

(2nd edit., 1949, Pitmans, p. 60)

But whereas the Renaissance introduced the despotic concepts of the revived Roman Civil Law, it did so in conjunction with a body of codified law of the highest technical quality based upon the immense practical achievements of the Roman people. Austinian jurisprudence, however, introduced no body of established law, it introduces no code, but merely a doctrine totally destructive of the principle of law derived from the consent of the people. Austinian jurisprudence established the monstrosity of a doctrine of lawlessness as the foundation of law, which can only result in the total destruction of all civilised existence.

THE AGE OF PROGRESS AND REFORM

The modern age was initiated in England by the Parliamentary Reform Act of 1832, the real significance of which lay not in the reform of popular representation in the House of Commons but, according to Dicey:-

> "...in its effect upon public opinion. Reform thus regarded was revolution. It altered the way in which people thought of the Constitution and taught Englishmen once and for all that venerable institutions which custom had made unchangeable could easily and without violence be changed. It gave authority to the democratic creed and fostered the conviction or delusion that the will of the nation could be expressed only through elected representatives."
>
> (Law and Public Opinion in England, A. V. Dicey, 1905, p. 42)

The forces which the Reform Act of 1832 brought to power were the Benthamite Utilitarian and the Philosophic Radical movements. These were the English and Scottish outcrop of the French Enlightenment which prepared the ground for the French Revolution of the 18th century. French Enlightenment dealt with the social and political conditions in France (and on the continent) created by the reception of the Roman Civil code in relation to the mercantile developments which preceded the Industrial Revolution. This had produced a new wealthy mercantile middle class in France which resented the stagnant and sterile social, economic and political conditions created by the hereditary despotisms established by the Lex Regia of the Civil Code which allowed the dried-up remnants of the medieval social order to survive. In this, a small effete aristocratic privileged class enjoyed their medieval rights without any corresponding duties, and a large dispossessed class were loaded with medieval duties without any corresponding rights by which the duties were originally balanced.

In this effete hereditary social order, the new prosperous middle class found itself relegated with the dispossessed masses and excluded from political and social participation. They found their mercantile and industrial activities hampered and obstructed by medieval laws and customs which they were powerless to alter. They, therefore, challenged the whole basis of this system of authority and posed the doctrine that it is from the will of the people and not from the will of a hereditary ruler that all authority should be derived. This basis of modern democracy was received throughout the continent of Europe as the beginning of the age of reason and the rights of man and as the basis of progress and reform.

The mercantile classes, however, saw the age of progress in the terms of their own mercantile experience based on the pursuit of personal gain. Their aim was to establish a social system in which the principle of self interest, as expounded by the new science of political economy, could be imposed regardless of the human consequences. The new working classes which the industrial revolution was creating were expected to accept this economic system in which the medieval master and servant relationship had already been destroyed by the Civil Law with its principle of free contract. In consequence, the working classes were to be regarded as the purveyors of labour as an economic commodity subject to the law of supply and demand, and suffer the consequences in poverty, unemployment and general insecurity without any social rights.

To impose such an economic system upon any community required dictatorial powers, and this the Roman code provided especially as it included the Patria Potestas of family regulation by an extension of which the owners of the individual enterprises were established as complete dictators owning no responsibility to the community.

Before, however, the fundamental conflict between the human claims of the working classes and the mercantile principle of personal gain and self interest became apparent, the cause of democracy had widespread support in its general promise of human emancipation and social progress.

French political democracy, with its appeal to the will of the people as the sole basis of all authority, was a purely abstract concept. For practical purposes, as a basis of law and government, there is no such thing as the will of the people. In consequence, French Revolutionary ideology had to adopt an artificial process by which the will of the people could be established. In place of the Lex Regia, it propounded the Lex Majoris Partis, which was merely the Lex Regia in a new guise. In this, any minority, however large, was considered to have surrendered all rights unconditionally into the control of the majority, however small. The establishment of a majority required political organisation in the form of political parties. As, however, the majority was thus invested with the sovereignty of the people, this sovereignty could not be controlled by any fundamental law, and in consequence, no determined rule could be enforced as to how this all powerful majority was to be legally established. This had to be left entirely to the free play of political forces as expressed by the political party organisations in which the mercantile classes, by their financial resources, could weald an absolute power.

The central feature of French Revolutionary democracy was a majority dictatorship determined by party organisation vested with the sovereign authority previously exercised by the hereditary monarch.

French Revolutionary democracy was generated by an intellectual activity known as the Enlightenment, which aimed to inspire and direct this new social system.

Alexis de Tocqueville, the author of the classic on American democracy, left a penetrating insight into the nature of French Enlightenment which he publicised in 1856 under the translated title of "The State of Society in France before the Revolution of 1789". In chapter XV, entitled "That the French aimed at Reform before Liberty", he wrote:-

> "It is worthy of observation that amongst all the ideals and all the feelings which led to the French Revolution, the idea and the taste for political liberty, properly so called, were the last to manifest themselves and the first to disappear...

> Towards the middle of the eighteenth century, a certain number of writers began to appear who devoted themselves especially to questions of public administration, and who were designated in consequence of several principles they held in common by the general name of Political Economists or Physiocrats. These economists have left less

conspicuous traces in history than the French philosophers; perhaps they contributed less to the approach of the Revolution; yet I think the true character of the Revolution may best be studied in their works. The French philosophers confined themselves for the most part to very general and very abstract opinions on government; the economists without abandoning their theory, clung more closely to the facts. The former said what might be thought, the latter sometimes pointed out what might be done. All the institutions which the Revolution was about to annihilate were the peculiar objects of their attacks, none found favour in their sight. All the institutions, on the contrary which may be regarded as the product of the Revolution, were announced beforehand by these economical writers, and ardently recommended; there is hardly one of these institutions of which the germ may not be discovered in some of their writings; and those writings may be said to contain all that is most substantial in the Revolution itself. Nay, more, their books already bore the stamp of that Revolutionary and democratic temper which we know so well; they breath not only the hatred of certain privileges but even diversity was odious to them, they would adore equality even in servitude. All that thwarted their designs is to be crushed. They care little for plighted faith, nothing for private rights - or rather, to speak accurately, private rights have already ceased in their eyes to exist- public utility is everything. Yet these were men for the most part of gentle, peaceful lives, worthy persons, upright magistrates, able administrators but the peculiar spirit of their task bore them on.

The past was to these economists a subject of endless contempt. 'This nation has been governed for centuries on false principle' said Letronne, 'everything seems to have been done by haphazard'. Starting from this notion, they set to work; no institution was so ancient or so well established in the history of France that they hesitated to demand its suppression from the moment it incommoded them or deranged the symmetry of their plans. One of these writers proposed to obliterate at once all the ancient territorial divisions of the kingdom and to change all the names of the provinces, forty years before the constituent assembly executed the scheme.

They had already conceived the idea of all the social and administrative reforms which the Revolution has accomplished before the idea of free institutions had begun to cross their minds. They were extremely favourable to the free exchange of produce and to the doctrine of Laissez Faire et Laissez Passer, the basis of free trade and free labour; but as for political liberties, properly so called, these did not occur to their minds, or if perchance they did occur to their imaginations, such ideas were at once rejected. Most of them began to display considerable hostility to deliberative assemblies, to local and secondary powers and, in general to all the checks which have been established at different times, in all free nations, to balance the central power of the government. 'The system of checks' said Quesnay 'is a fatal idea in government'. 'The speculations in which a system of checks has been devised are chimerical' said a friend of the same writer...

To accomplish the revolution which they contemplated ...it seemed to them more easy and more proper to make the administrative power of the Crown itself the instrument of their designs.

That new administrative power has not sprung from the institutions of the Middle Ages nor did it bear the mark of that period; in spite of its errors they discovered in it some beneficial tendencies. Like themselves it was naturally favourable to equality of conditions and to uniformity of rules; as much as themselves it cordially detested all the ancient powers which were born of feudalism or tended to aristocracy. In all Europe no machine of government existed so well organised, so vast, so strong. To find such a government ready to their hands seemed to them a most fortunate circumstance; they would have called it providential, if it had been the fashion then, as it now is, to cause providence to intervene on all occasions. 'The state of France', said Letronne is infinitely better than that of England, for here reforms can be accomplished which will change the whole condition of the country in a moment whilst amongst the English such reforms may always be thwarted by political parties'.

The point was then not to destroy this absolute power but to convert it. 'The state must govern according to the rules of essential order' said Mercier de la Riviere 'and when this is the case it ought to be all powerful'. 'Let the state thoroughly understand its duty and then let it be altogether free', from Quesnay to the Abbe Bodeau, they were all of the same mind. They not only relied on the Royal administration, to reform the social conditions of their own age, but they partially borrowed from it the idea of the future government they hoped to found. The latter was framed in the image of the former.

These economists held that it is the business of the state not only to command the nation, but to fashion it in a certain manner, to form the character of the population upon a certain preconceived model, to inspire the mind with such opinions and the heart with such sentiments as it may deem necessary. In fact they set no limits to the rights of the state, nor to what it could effect. The state was not only to reform men, but to transform them - perhaps if it chose to make others. 'The state can make men what it pleases,' said Bodeau. That proposition includes all their theories.

This unlimited social power which the French economists had conceived was not only greater than

136

any power they ever beheld, but it differed from every other power by its origin and nature. It did not flow directly from the Deity, it did not rest on tradition; it was an impersonal power; It was not called the King but the State; and it was not the inheritance of a family but the product and the representative of all. It entitled them to bend the right of every man to the will of the rest.

That peculiar form of tyranny which is called Democratic Despotism and which was utterly unknown to the Middle Ages, was already familiar to these writers. No gradations in society, no distinction of classes, no fixed ranks - a people composed of individuals nearly alike and entirely equal - this confused mass being recognised as the only legitimate sovereign, but carefully deprived of all the faculties which would enable it either to direct or even superintend its own government. Above this mass a single officer, charged to do everything its own name without consulting it. To control this officer, public opinion deprived of its organs; to arrest him revolutions but no laws. In principle a subordinate agent; in fact a master."

(Trans. H. Reeve, 3rd. Edit., p.136)

The intellectual activity which produced this despotic ideology saw itself as the great movement for progress and reform, and established an abstract intellectualism as the dominant influence in the political development of the whole of the western world in the 19th century extending into the 20th. It reached its horrific climax in the totalitarian dictatorships and, in particular in the Nazi Party dictatorship in Germany.

The outstanding feature of French Revolutionary ideology is a total rejection of all tradition and past experience.

Mallet du Pain, whom the French historian Taine regarded as one of the few people who understood the significance of the French Revolution in his "Mercure Britannique", as quoted by Professor Willert in the Cambridge Modern History, declared:-

"Philosophy may boast her reign over the country she has devastated. Her votaries hastened the degeneration and corruption of the French by weakening the bulwarks of morality, by sophisticating conscience and by substituting the uncertain dictates of man's fallible reason, the equivocation of passion and of selfishness, for rules of duty imposed by tradition, confirmed by education and secured by habit. They threw doubts on all truths, and shook the foundation of whatever had been established and consecrated by time, by experience and by a wisdom saner than their own. Intellectual anarchy paved the way for social anarchy. Rousseau the favourite author of the middle classes who was read and commented upon in the streets, misled virtue itself. He taught the notion to receive the dogmas of popular sovereignty and of natural equality as axioms and deduced from them their most extreme consequences. He was the prophet of the Revolution and his works were gospel."

(Vol VIII, The French Revolution, Ch. 1. Philosophy and the Revolution)

Sir Henry Sumner Maine, in his essay "Popular Government", published in 1885, summarised the teachings of Rousseau. He pointed out:-

"A vastly more formidable conception bequeathed to us by Rousseau is that of the omnipotent democratic state rooted in natural rights; the state which has at its disposal everything which individual men value, their property, their persons and their independence; the State which is bound to respect neither precedent nor prescription; The State which may make laws for its subjects ordering what they will drink or eat and in what way they shall spend their earnings...Some particles of Rousseau's thought may be discovered in the mental atmosphere of his time. 'Natural Law' and 'Natural Rights' are phrases properly belonging to a theory not of politics but of jurisprudence which originating from the Roman jurisconsults had great attraction for the lawyers of France. The despotic sovereign of the 'Contract Social'. the all powerful community is an inverted copy of the King of France...The omnipotent democracy is the king proprietor, the lord of all men's fortunes and persons but it is the French King turned upside down."

It was this political, social, legal, and democratic despotism which the Benthamite movement Utilitarians and Phylosophic Radicals had propagated in England long before the outbreak of the revolution in France and which, by winning power in the reformed Parliament after 1832, they imposed upon the British people.

The fundamental principle which actuated the Benthamite movement was "Laissez Faire", which aimed to establish the freedom of the individual to pursue unhampered his own selfish interests regardless of social and political consequences. In English Common Law, every right and liberty of the individual was subject to a counterbalancing duty by which the rights and liberties of fellow subjects were safeguarded and thus, the social balance of the community was preserved. Benthamite liberty abolished these counterbalancing duties, which were regarded as infringements on the liberty to pursue uninhibited selfish interests. In this, the Benthamite movement destroyed the basic concept of political and civil liberty, which rested on the fundamental right of every freeborn Englishman to ventilate and obtain redress for his social and political grievances. Under the Benthamite concept of liberty, there could be no legal redress for such grievances as everyone powerful enough was given the right to exploit his fellow subjects by every and any means short of petty criminality.

To this end, the Benthamites removed the development of English law away from the judicial process by which it had become the greatest system of jurisprudence since the Roman republic to the process of Parliamentary legislation established by partisan politicians.

As Henry Sumner Maine pointed out in 1885 in his essays on "Popular Government" under the title of "The Age of Progress":-

"The English Parliament...legislated very little until fifty years since, when it fell under the influence of Bentham and his disciples. Ever since the first Reform Act however the volume of legislation has been increasing..."

(Page 148)

"The materials for legislation are being constantly supplied in ever increasing abundance through the competition of Parties...and is the chief reason of the general impression that ours is an age of progress to be indefinitely continued..."

(Page 151)

Dicey, in his "Law and Opinion of England" tells us:-

"The guides of English legislation, during the era of individualism, by whatever party name they were known, accepted the fundamental ideas of Benthamism, the ultimate end, therefore, of those men was to promote legislation in accordance with the principle of utility; but their immediate and practical object was the extension of individual liberty as the proper means of ensuring the greatest happiness of the greatest number. Their policy was however thwarted by the opposition or inertness of classes biased by some sinister interest. Hence sincere believers in Laissez Faire found that for the attainments of their ends, the improvement and the strengthening of government machinery was an absolute necessity."

(Page 305)

As Dicey remarks in the same work:-

"Benthamism thus led to the demand for such a reform in the constitution of Parliament, as should make it a fit instrument for carrying out Benthamite ideas."

(Page 166)

This was achieved by converting Parliament into a sovereign instrument of legislation.

Though the doctrine of Parliamentary sovereignty was only formulated in 1885 by A. V. Dicey in his "Law of the Constitution", it was, however, a basic Benthamite assumption for over half a century previously. As Dicey himself pointed out in "Law and Opinion in England":-

> "Parliamentary sovereignty...treated as a reality by Bentham was an instrument well adapted for the establishment of democratic despotism."

> (Page 304)

Instead of a supreme Parliament, which operated by advice and consent, a sovereign Parliament gave the Benthamite movement an instrument of will and command by which they could impose their ideas as law.

This is in fact, what was achieved, for as Dicey put it:-

> "Benthamite legislation...might seem to be dictated by the will of a despotic sovereign inspired with the spirit of Bentham."

> (Page 183)

Thus, Benthamism nullified the legal foundations of the English Parliamentary constitution.

Professor Gough, in his study entitled "Fundamental Law in English Constitutional History", heads his bibliography with the note:-

> "The idea of fundamental law was so ubiquitous and so long lived in English history that it would be vain to attempt to compile a list of primary authorities."

> (Page 222)

In his main work, however, he records that:-

"It was with the Benthamite principle of utility, accompanied by the introduction of Parliamentary Reform, that modernity really began to make itself felt. Then at last the relics of the idea of fundamental law gave way before the realisation that there was nothing to hinder the possessors of power from using it to promote their own interests and that how to do so most successfully is the art of politics."

(Page 191)

This set the basis of modern political democracy as the struggle of sectional interests for their own selfish ends under cover of a freedom of opinion in the form of party politics. As Dicey pointed out in "Law and Opinion in England.":-

"Were we to assume that the persons who have power to make law are solely and wholly influenced by the desire to promote their own personal and selfish interest, yet their view of their interest and, therefore, their legislation must be determined by their opinion."

(Page 14)

Opinion of the powerful interests was from now on to be the supreme and final arbiter of English law and government.

The impact of Benthamite progress and reform on English society has been recorded in the memorable words of a future Prime Minister, Benjamin Disraeli, in his novel, "Sybil" (Book1, Chap. 5) published in 1845:-

"Since the passing of the Reform Act the altar of Mammon has blazed with triple worship. To acquire, to accumulate, to plunder each other by virtue of philosophic phrases, to propose a Utopia to consist only of wealth and toil, this has been the breathless business of enfranchised England for the last twelve years until we are startled from our voracious strife by the wail of intolerable serfage."

In the early Chartist movement, we see the expression of resentment of the English people not only at the brutality of the new industrialism but at the loss of ancient rights which the Benthamite age swept away. The spirit of this resentment can be seen in the words of Joseph Rayner Stephens (convicted of sedition and sentenced to 18 months' imprisonment) when he spoke at Heartshead Moor on October 15th 1838:-

> "We stand upon our old rights - we seek no change - we say, give us the good old laws of England unchanged. They shall not be changed, the laws of our forefathers; and what are those laws? 'Magna Carta'. The good old laws of English freedom - freedom of speech - freedom of workshops - freedom of homesteads - free and happy firesides and no workhouses...give no heed to men who teach new fangled politics - French politics - politico economical politics - stick to the good old laws, the good old laws of England."

(State Trials (N.S.) Vol. 3, Col. 1223)

Once the Benthamite movement had firmly established its grip on Parliament, it was no longer necessary to maintain the pretences that it represented the progressive development of individual liberty and its character could be revealed in the setting up of the autocratic, democratic state along the lines of French Revolutionary ideology.

This was recorded by Dicey in "Law and Opinion in England" when he tells us:-

> "The Liberals then of 1830 were themselves zealots for individual freedom but they entertained beliefs, which, though the men that held them knew it not, might well under altered conditions, foster the despotic authority of a democratic state. The effect actually produced by a system of thought does not depend on the intention of its originators; ideas which have once obtained general acceptance work out their own logical results under the control mainly of events. Somewhere between 1868 and 1900 changes took place which brought into prominence the authoritative side of Benthamite

> Liberalism. Faith in Laissez Faire suffered an eclipse;
> hence the principle of utility became an argument in
> favour, not of individual freedom but of the absolutism
> of the state."

(Page 308)

The true character of this new order is shown by Dicey when he declared that:-

> "It is absolutely certain that utilitarian reforms...have
> often been achieved in defiance of popular sentiment."

(Page 447)

At no time were the English people made aware of the constitutional revolution which was being carried through (by no legal or constitutional process) in the cause of French political democracy. The forms, institutions and ceremonies of the Parliamentary constitution were solemnly preserved to disguise the fact that the Parliamentary constitution had been totally violated.

The first notification that any basic changes had been effected was given by Walter Bagehot in 1867 when he published "The English Constitution". Here he pointed out that:-

> "...the appendages of the monarchy have been converted
> into the essence of a republic: only here, because of a
> more numerous heterogeneous population, it is needful
> to keep the ancient show while we secretly interpolate
> the new reality."

(World Classics CCCXXX, p. 253)

How little the people of England were aware of what was proceeding can be seen in Bagehot's assertion that the chief function of the English monarchy was nothing more to:-

> "...act as a disguise. It enables our real rulers to change
> without heedless people knowing it. The masses of
> Englishmen are not fit for an elective government;

if they knew how near they were to it, they would be surprised and almost tremble."

(Ibid. p. 48)

The constitutional changes which could not be disguised were represented to the English people to be the results of the progressive development of a long drawn-out saga of English constitutional progress from a royal despotism to a free democracy.

As Dicey recorded in "Law and Opinion in England":-

> "Legislative utilitarianism is nothing else than systematised individualism and individualism has always found its natural home in England.
>
> During the long conflicts which have made up the constitutional history of England, individualism has meant hatred of the arbitrary prerogatives of the Crown, or in other words, of the collective and autocratic authority of the state and has fostered the instinctive and strenuous effort to secure for the humblest Englishman the rule of law. Benthamism was, and was ultimately felt to be little else than the logical and systematic development of those individual rights and especially of that individual freedom which has always been dear to the Common Law of England. The faith indeed of the utilitarians in the supreme value of individual liberty and the assumption which that faith rests, owe far more to the traditions of Common Law than thinkers such as John Mill, who was no lawyer, are prepared to acknowledge. Bentham is heavily indebted to Coke and utilitarianism has inherited some of its most valuable ideas from Puritanism."

(Page 174)

This falsification and misrepresentation of English constitutional history began immediately with the rise of Benthamite influence in 1832. It can be clearly recognised even in a historian of the standing of Macaulay.

In 1828 before the full impact of Benthamism had made itself felt Macauley declared:-

> "The Constitution of England was only one of a large family. In all the monarchies of western Europe during the Middle Ages, there existed restraints on the royal authority, fundamental laws and representative assemblies. In the fifteenth century the government of Castile seems to have been as free as that of our own country. That of Aragon was beyond all question more so. In France the sovereign was more absolute. Yet even the States-General could constitutionally impose taxes and at the very time when the authority of these assemblies was beginning to languish, the Parliament of Paris received such an accession of strength as established it in some measure to perform the function of a legislative assembly. Sweden and Denmark had constitutions of a similar description.
>
> Let us overlap two or three hundred years and contemplate Europe, at the commencement of the eighteenth century. Every free constitution save one has gone down. That of England has weathered the danger and was riding in full security."
>
> (Critical and Historical essays, Essays on Hallam, Sept. 1828, p. 69)

In the highly emotional conditions generated by the Benthamites in the period of Parliamentary Reform, such conceptions of English constitutional achievement were discarded as old-fashioned and reactionary.

In 1835 under the full blast of progress and reform of the Benthamite utilitarian movement, Macauley expressed a completely new approach which was to set the tone of the constitutional history of England to meet the requirements of the new age. Macaulay declared:-

> "The history of England is emphatically the history of progress. It is the history of a constant movement of the public mind, of a constant change in the institutions of

a great society. We see this society at the beginning of the twelfth century in a state more miserable than the state in which the most degraded nations of the east now are. We see it subjected to the tyranny of a handful of armed foreigners...In the course of seven centuries the wretched and degraded race have become the greatest and most highly civilised people that ever the world saw."

(Critical and Historical essays, Essay on Sir James Mackintosh, July, 1836, p. 322)

Here we have Macaulay, the Whig, who believed that the laws of England were the birthright of the people thereof, converted into the new Radical Liberal who sees all in terms of progress, in which the laws of England were the relics of a dark reactionary age. How this was so can be seen in the words of William Massey, the Liberal historian, in his "History of England" when he wrote:-

"For what is the strict law of our boasted constitution? The sovereign can do no wrong; he is absolutely irresponsible; he can make war and peace at his own will; he can appoint and dismiss all his principal ministers both civil and military together with most of the most subordinate public servants at his pleasure. He can impose an absolute veto upon any law which the other two branches of the legislature have passed ever so often. He can dissolve Parliament when he will. He can at any time command a majority in one House of Parliament by the creation of legislators for life or with hereditary succession. He has the direct nomination of one class, the Lords Spiritual of that assembly. These are the unquestioned privileges and prerogatives of the Crown and make the sovereign of Great Britain on paper at least equal in power with the most absolute monarch in Europe."

(History of England during the Reign of George III, 2nd Edit. 1865, Vol. III, p. 393)

From Royal despotism to democracy is the theme of our modern history textbooks. In his "History of England", Professor G. M. Trevelyan, in dealing with Magna Carta, tells us:-

> "A king has been brought to order not by a posse of reactionary feudalists but by the community of land under baronial leadership. A tyrant had been subjected to the laws which hitherto it had been his privilege to administer and modify at will. A process had begun which was to end in putting the power of the Crown into the hands of the community at large."

(Page 171)

A similar approach to English constitutional history is apparent in Walter Bagehot's "The English Constitution", which has been summarised by R. H. S. Crossman in the latest edition of "The English Constitution", in the introduction of which Mr. Crossman writes:-

> "This new constitution, says Bagehot, is only the most recent state in a long historical process. For hundreds of years the efficient and dignified parts of the constitution were united in the persons of the King. Britain was ruled by absolute monarchy - a type of government intelligible to the simplest minds. The absolute monarchy was gradually replaced by constitutional monarchy in which sovereignty was divided between the king and the landed aristocracy with the House of Commons exerting some checks as the representative of the popular will and finally in the years since 1832, constitutional monarchy has given way to a disguised republic."

(Fontana Library, 1963, p. 15)

Whatever we can gather from this farrago of historic nonsense, the fact is that this disguised republic embodies the principles of state absolutism by which the Benthamite movement replaced our free Parliamentary constitution. This was formulated by Dicey under the doctrine of Parliamentary sovereignty, which he himself described as an instrument well adapted for the establishment of democratic despotism. Dicey claimed this to be a principle of the English Constitution but the only authority to which he could appeal was the attempt to establish a royal parliamentary despotism in the early years of the reign of George III.

In "The Law and the Constitution", he wrote:-

> "Anyone who studies the questions connected with the name of John Wilkes or the disputes between England and the American colonies will see that George the Third and the great majority of George the Third's statesmen maintained up to 1784 a view of Parliamentary sovereignty which made Parliament in the strictest sense the sovereign power. To this theory Fox clung both in his youth as a Tory and in his later life as a Whig. The greatness of Chatham and his son lay in their perceiving that behind the Crown, behind the Revolution Families, behind Parliament itself , lay what Chatham calls "the Great Public" and what we should call the nation, and that on the will of the nation depended the authority of Parliament.".

(10th edit., p. 435)

Whatever support Dicey may find among the statesmen who led the country into the catastrophe of the American war for his doctrine of Parliamentary sovereignty, he cannot include among these either Fox or Chatham. Their total repudiation of any such doctrine is clear in their speeches. For example, Fox speaking in the House of Commons in his later life as a Whig and as a champion of the French Revolution, on December 3rd, 1795, declared:-

> "I am ready therefore to repeat the doctrine I have stated to its full extent and I will repeat that neither lords nor Commons nor king, no, nor the whole legislature together are to be considered as possessing the power to enslave the people of this country. They might separately or unitedly to such acts as might justify resistance from the people. Is this doctrine false?

Is it necessary to urge any argument to its truth? It is the doctrine I have learnt from my early youth."

Parliamentary History of England (Hansard), Vol. XXXII, Col. 454 & 385)

Exactly the same point was made by Chatham, who, speaking in the House of Lords on January 22nd, 1770, declared:-

"I have been bred up in these principles (of the English Constitution) and I know that, when the liberty of the subject is invaded and all redress denied him, resistance is justified."

(Ibid. Vol. XVI, Col. 748)

Chatham was the outstanding champion of English Constitutional law as against the lawless concepts inherent in the doctrine of Parliamentary sovereignty. Among many of his speeches, we have the one he made in the House of Lords on January 9th,1770. Chatham declared:-

"My Lords, I thought the slavish doctrine of passive obedience had long since been exploded and when our Kings were obliged to confess that their title to the Crown and the rule of their government had no other foundation than the known laws of the land, I never expected to hear a divine right or a divine infallibility attributed to any other branch of the legislature...I am a plain man and I have been brought up with a religious reverence for the original simplicity of the laws of England. By what sophistry they have been perverted, by what artifice they have been involved in obscurity is not for me to explain; the principles however, of the English laws are still sufficiently clear; they are founded in reason, and are the masterpiece of the human understanding; but it is in the text that I would look for a direction of my judgement, not in the commentators of modern professors.

The noble lord (Mansfield) assures us that he knows not in what code the law of Parliament is to be found;

that the House of Commons, when they act as judges , have no law to direct them but their own wisdom; that their decisions are law and if they determine wrong the subject has no appeal but to heaven. What then my Lords, are all the generous efforts of our ancestors, are all those glorious contentions, by which they meant to secure themselves and to transmit to their posterity a known law, a certain rule of living reduced to this conclusion, that instead of an arbitrary power of a King we must submit to the arbitrary power of the House of Commons. If this be true what benefit do we derive from the exchange? Tyranny, my Lords, is detestable in every shape but in none so formidable as when it is assumed and exercised by a number of tyrants. But, my lords, this is not the fact, this is not the Constitution; we have a law of Parliament, we have a code in which any honest man may find it, We have Magna Carta, we have the Statute Book and the Bill of Rights."

(Parliamentary History of England (Hansard) Vol. XVI, Col. 658)

The Parliamentary Constitution, which Chatham, Fox and Burke were upholding, restored in 1784 on the defeat of George III, was the object of the attack by the Benthamite revolution set in motion by the Parliamentary Reform Act of 1832 and which led to the establishment of the Party Cabinet system under the name of Parliamentary Government. As Dicey pointed out in "Law and Opinion in England":-

"In 1832 passionate enthusiasm for Parliamentary Reform and all the innovations to which it gave birth, displaced as it were in a moment the obstinate Toryism for which nearly half a century has been accepted creed if not of the whole nation, yet assuredly of the governing classes; here we have a revolution in popular opinion of which the violence was equalled by its suddenness."

(Page 31)

No one could have given greater support to this revolution than Dicey himself, who by his "Law of the Constitution" provided it with a constitutional basis on which it still rests. But no one could have condemned the consequences of this revolution more outspokenly than Dicey himself.

In his introduction to the 8th edition of "The Law and the Constitution", Dicey recorded that:-

> "Parliamentary government has by its continued existence betrayed two defects hardly suspected by the liberals or Reformers of Europe or at any rate of England between 1832 and 1880. We now know for certain that while popular government may be, under wise leadership, a good machine for simply destroying existing evils, it may turn out a very poor instrument for the construction of new institutions or the realisation of new ideals. We know further that party government, which to many among the wisest of modern constitutionalists, appear to be the essence of England's far famed constitution, inevitably gives rise to partisanship and at last produces a machine which may well lead to political corruption, and may when this evil is escaped, lead to the strange but acknowledged result that a not unfairly elected legislature may misrepresent the permanent will of the electors."

Here we have the final judgement on the Age of Progress and reform which has taken from us our great Parliamentary heritage. Nothing now remains that can justify the constitutional revolution which the Benthamites initiated in the reformed Parliament after 1832 and which has resulted in the Party Cabinet establishing its lawless usurpation over the constitutional authority of the British people.

THE CORRUPTION OF ENGLISH LAW

The corruption of English law is the final legacy left us by the age of Progress and Reform of the 19th century. Law in England today rests solely on the will and command of the secret Party Cabinet, suitably processed for legal purposes by the party packed House of Commons under the name of Parliament. The application of Austin sovereignty to Parliament not only destroyed the legal supremacy of Parliament but destroyed the very roots of English Common Law as derived from the consent of the people.

In place of the free system of English law, we now have Austinian jurisprudence.

As Sir Carlton Allen points out in his work "Law in the making":-

> "Many a student must feel that he reads Austin only in order to confute him, yet Austinian jurisprudence, despite all the broadsides and notwithstanding the further disadvantages of an unattractive manner of presentation, so far maintains its influence that it may still be described as the characteristic jurisprudence of England."

> (2nd edit., p. 7)

The full implications of Austinian jurisprudence can best be gauged from the words of Austin himself. In his sixth lecture, Austin declared:-

> "Political and civil liberty has been erected into an idol and extolled with extravagant praise by doting and fanatical worshippers. To the ignorant and bawling fanatics who stun you with their pother about liberty political and civil liberty seems to be the principle end for which government ought to exist. But the final cause or purpose for which government ought to exist,

is the furtherance of the Commonwealth to the greatest possible extent."

(Province of Jurisprudence Determined, 2nd edit., p.242)

In the same lecture, Austin laid it down categorically that:-

"Every supreme government is free from legal restraint. Every supreme government is legally despotic. The distinction of government into free and despotic can hardly mean ...that the subjects of the government which are denominated free, are protected against their governments by positive law. Nor can it mean that the governments which are denominated free, leave or grant to their subjects more political liberty than those which are styled despotic. For the epithet free importing praise and the epithet despotic importing blame, they who distinguish governments into free and despotic suppose that the first are better than the second. But in as much as political liberty may be generally useful or pernicious we cannot infer that a government is better than another government, because of the sum of the liberties which are left to its subjects by the latter. The excess of the sum of the liberties which the former leaves to its subjects may be purely mischievous. It may consist of freedom from restraints which are required by the common weal; and which the government would lay upon its subjects, if it fulfilled its duties of the Deity."

(Page 244)

Such is now the principle of law and government under the Party Cabinet system.

Under the doctrine of Austinian sovereignty, there is no recognition whatsoever of those fundamental human rights derived from the law of Nature, which lord Kilmuir, then lord Chancellor, described in 1957 to the 80th Convention of the American Bar Association in Westminster hall as one of the noblest conceptions in the history of jurisprudence. (The Times, July, 25th, 1957). It was the law of Nature which enabled the Roman civilian lawyer to mitigate the worst excess of despotic and arbitrary power which the tenets of the Civil Law otherwise legalised. In the Law of Nature, the Roman lawyer and the common lawyer could to a great extent, reach an understanding. As Blackstone in the "Commentaries on the Laws of England" described it:-

> "This law of nature being coeval with mankind, and dictated by God himself is of course superior in obligation to any other. It is binding all over the globe in all countries and at all times; no human laws are of any validity if contrary to this, and such of them as are valid, derive all their force and all their authority mediately and immediately, from this original."

(Vol. 1, S. 11, p. 41)

Blackstone further declared:-

> "Those rights which God and nature have established are therefore called natural rights, such as are life and liberty, need not the aid of human laws to be more effectually invested in every man than they are; neither do they give any additional strength when declared by the municipal laws to be inviolable. On the contrary no human legislature has power to bridge or destroy them, unless the owner himself commits some act that amount to forfeiture."

(Ibid., p.54)

This great concept of law has now been stamped out by Austinian jurisprudence. As Eastwood and Keeton point out in their manual "The Austinian Theories of Law and Sovereignty":-

> "The idea of law and nature, at one time so popular in England, has been altogether abolished from English thought. Since Austin's time, no responsible writer has said as Blackstone once did, "The Law of Nature is binding all over the globe in all countries; no human laws are of any validity if contrary to this"

(Page 23)

How far this can go under Austinian sovereignty as applied to Parliament, Dicey himself indicates when he quotes the work of his cousin, Leslie Stephen, "Science and Ethics", where he writes:-

> "If a legislature decided that all blue eyed babies should be murdered, the preservation of blue eyed babies would be illegal, but legislatures must go mad before they could pass such a law and subjects idiotic before they could submit to it."

(Law of the Constitution, 8th edit., p. 79)

We now know in the totalitarian excesses of our times that there is no such political limitation to the legal authority of a sovereign power uncontrolled by law. If a sovereign Parliament has a legal authority to murder blue eyed babies, then it has the legal authority to do anything else in the destruction of human rights and can destroy just about anyone at any time, for any or no reason, in any way. If there is such a power in law, there is also power to set up secret police with secret courts to enforce any barbarous edicts against the conscience of mankind.

In our age, we have had to learn the great and terrible lessons of the past that lawless government can be one of the most brutal forces which man can suffer. We have seen in our generation the long, costly, and untiring efforts of all the forces of civilisation to establish law to restrain the activities of sovereign rulers. We have sent to the gallows German and Japanese leaders who infringed no positive law or even declared law. We relied on our innermost conviction that there is a Law of Nature based upon common justice and right and which every man in his conscience knows and recognises. At an immense cost of human lives and suffering, we have re-affirmed the principle that this law of civilisation may not be infringed by the mere will of any rulers.

This was the issue which was settled at the trial of the German rulers at Nuremberg at the close of the Second World War. In those trials, English lawyers played a decisive and leading part. How did they deal with the Austinian doctrine of a sovereignty above all law?

Sir Hartley Shawcross, K. C., M. P. (as he was then), the English Attorney General and the Chief British Prosecutor, denounced Austinian theory as small town lawyer stuff. In his opening address to the International Military Tribunal on December 4th, 1945, he declared:-

> "There are, it is very true, some small town lawyers who deny the very existence of any International Law and indeed, as I have said, the rules of the Law of Nations may not satisfy the Austinian test of being imposed by a sovereign. But the legal regulation of international relation rests upon quite a different juridical foundation. It depends upon the consent, but a consent which once given cannot be withdrawn by unilateral action. In the international field, the source of law is not the command of a sovereign, but by the treaty agreement binding upon every State which had adhered to it."

> (The Trial of the German War Criminals, Opening Speeches, H. M. S. Stationery Office, 1946, p. 56)

Why there should be a distinction between international law and any other kind of law was not explained, nor is it obvious. If in the international field, the source of law is the treaty of agreement upon every state which had adhered, is not Parliament bound by the treaty of union between the sovereign kingdoms of England and Scotland. How, then, can Parliament be sovereign? Whatever the distinction may be, if there is any, the fact remains that only by a repudiation of Austinian theory was it possible for the war criminals to be prosecuted at all by the English lawyers. With this repudiation of Austin, there arises immediately the great conception of fundamental law - a constitutional law of a world order expressed in the Charter of the United Nations. Here it is that Lord Shawcross gave us, in resounding words, the meaning of the Rule of Law:-

> "History - very recent history - does not warrant the view that a state cannot be criminal. On the other hand, the immeasurable potentialities for evil inherent in the State in this age of science and organisation would seem to demand quite imperatively means of repression of criminal conduct even more drastic and more effective

than in the case of individuals. And so far, therefore, as this Charter has put on record, the principle of criminal responsibility of the State, it must be applauded as a wise and farseeing measure of international legislation. It is here that the Powers who framed the Charter took a step which justice, sound legal sense and an enlightened appreciation of the good of mankind must acclaim without cavil or reserve. The Charter lays down expressly that there shall be individual responsibility for crimes against the peace committed on behalf of the State. The State is not an abstract entity . Its rights and duties are the rights and duties of men. Its actions are the actions of men. It is a salutary principle, a principle of law, that politicians who embark upon a particular policy, should not be able to seek immunity behind the intangible personality of the State. It is a salutary rule that persons who (violate law), should do so with a halter around their necks."

(Trial of the German War Criminals, Opening Speeches, H.M.S. O., 1946. P. 58)

In those magnificent sentences, Lord Shawcross was expressing the Rule of Law as it has been understood in England since the dawn of her history and upon which her whole Parliamentary constitution was founded. Is not the very reference to an International Charter as a fundamental law derived from the English Magna Carta, otherwise known as the Great Charter of English Liberties? But when it comes to modern England, these conditions no longer apply.

At the very time when the Nuremberg trials were in progress, Lord Shawcross informed an English audience:-

"Parliament is sovereign; it can make any laws. It could ordain that all blue eyed babies should be destroyed at birth, but it has been recognised that it is no good passing laws unless you can reasonably be sure that in the eventualities they contemplate, those laws will be supported and can be enforced."

(The Times, 13th May, 1946)

In nullifying all constitutional law, the doctrine of Austinian sovereignty has nullified the constitutional rights and liberties of the English people guaranteed by Magna Carta forever and confirmed in the great Parliamentary enactments such as the petition of Right, the Bill of Rights and the Act of Settlement though never repealed by Parliament.

According to Sir Ivor Jennings in "The Law and the Constitution,"-

> "Since Great Britain has no written constitution, there is no special protection for fundamental rights,"

(2nd edit., p. 40)

In Halsbury's "Laws of England", these rights and liberties are referred to as the "so called" liberties of the subject, and it is categorically declared:-

> "...since Parliament is sovereign the subject cannot possess guaranteed rights."

(2nd edit., Vol. VI. P.390)

Lord Wright, in his judgement Liversedge v. Anderson, which directly concerned the liberty of the subject, declared in the House of Lords:-

> "In the Constitution of England there are no guaranteed or absolute rights. The safeguard of British liberty is in the good sense of the people and in the system of representative and responsible government which has been evolved."

(All England Law Reports 1941, Vol. 3 House of Lords, 22n November, 1941.)

In England, the consequences of the doctrine of Austinian sovereignty can be seen in the series of Emergency Powers Acts of 1921, 1926, 1931 and 1939. The last, ostensibly a war measure, makes arbitrary imprisonment without a trial legal for the first time in English history, and it did so by authority of Parliament in those very terms which Parliament had condemned in the reign of Charles I. Lord Wright in the House of Lords judgement in the case of Liversedge v. Anderson said:-

"It may be objected that the discretionary powers thus vested in the Secretary of State are just those which were upheld by the Court of King's Bench in Darnel's Case and condemned in the Petition of Right. But the answer is that they are here lawful under this regulation because they are conferred not in general terms but under definite limitations by the supreme authority of Parliament and are thus the law of the land."

(All England Law Reports, 1941, Vol. 3, House of Lords, 22nd November, 1941, p. 403 H)

In wars previous to 1914, arbitrary powers were sanctioned by Parliament by the so called Habeas Corpus Suspension Acts. These suspension acts did not legalise any arrests, imprisonment or punishment, which was not lawful before the suspension acts were passed. The Habeas Corpus Suspension Acts merely made redress for the time being impossible, and an Act of Indemnity was required.

Dicey, in "The Law and the Constitution", explained that:-

"The Suspension Act, coupled with an Act of Indemnity does in truth arm the Executive with arbitrary powers. Still there are one or two considerations which limit the practical importance that can fairly be given to an expected Act of Indemnity. The relief to be obtained from it is prospective and uncertain. Any suspicion on the part of the public that officials had grossly abused their powers might make it difficult to obtain a parliamentary indemnity for things done while the Habeas Corpus Act was suspended. As regards the protection to be derived from the Act by men who have been guilty of irregular, illegal, oppressive or cruel conduct, everything depends upon the terms of the Act of Indemnity. These may be narrow or wide. The Indemnity Act, for instance, of 1801, gives very limited amount of protection to official wrongdoers."

(10th edit., p. 236)

Arbitrary imprisonment was introduced by Regulation 18B, made under the Emergency Powers Act of 1939 without the suspension of the Habeas Corpus Acts, and so made an act of indemnity unnecessary. The Government could act with the knowledge that it was fully protected in advance and that no actions for false imprisonment or harsh imprisonment could arise. The legal actions which did arise only served to confirm the powers claimed by the government, and these decisions now stand as precedents for all future occasions, both in times of peace and war, for any emergency, genuine or fabricated:-

Regulation 18B has established the following far reaching precedents in the working of any similar regulation in the future:-

(1) Any British subject, whatever his or her age, position or record may, upon secret information made by anyone, not on oath, be arrested and kept in prison without trial for an indefinite number of years.

(2) Such person has no appeal to anyone except to the person or official who ordered his imprisonment.

(3) No information as to the evidence upon which the imprisonment was ordered need be given to the prisoner nor is there any disclosure of the name of the secret informant.

(4) No means need be provided whereby the truth of the information can be established or rejected and the information itself need not even indicate an illegal activity. To be a relative or to be supposed to be a relative to someone can be sufficient grounds for imprisonment. All that is necessary is for someone to think he has reasonable grounds to believe something, and the necessary conditions for imprisonment are fulfilled.

(5) The subject can be imprisoned anywhere in England and may be taken from prison to prison under armed guard and handcuffed in a public conveyance.

(6) Despite assurances given to Parliament to the contrary, imprisonment can be oppressive and brutal without any legal redress even, such as is open to convicts and can include long periods of solitary confinement in dark cells with food limited to bread and water.

(7) The home and place of work of any subject may be searched in his or her absence and anything may be removed without the owner

being informed as to what has been removed, nor will anything so removed be necessarily ever returned to the legal owner.

(8) Anyone so arrested may be removed from his or her employment or office without any right of reinstatement compensation and any type of redress.

(9) Even in cases where imprisoned subjects are given a trial and are acquitted by verdict of the jury and discharged, they may still be kept in prison for years after such acquittal.

These points are not abstracted from Regulation 18B after an academic study of its wording. All these things did actually happen under Regulation 18B, and most of them were confirmed by decisions of the Courts. They all applied with equal force where acknowledged mistakes were made. As Sir Carleton Allen put it in his "Law and Orders", where he examines several cases that arose under Regulation 18B:-

> "I suggest that no Englishman can contemplate them with satisfaction. The general result is that no detainee has succeeded in obtaining any redress in any circumstances, even when he has been clearly wronged. Simultaneously, we have heard complacent assurances in high places that Magna Carta has remained intact throughout the war and that the Common Law is still the bulwark of our liberties. Reasonable persons and journals have justified all the severities of Reg. 18B as 'Acts of War' - a doctrine which implies that England has lived for five years under martial law and which betrays a significant decay of our constitutional principles. The notion that because a country is at war it has a right to commit 'Acts of War' on its own citizens is something never before heard of in our history...It is also worth remembering that this extreme expedient is not necessarily confined to war, but might re-appear even in time of peace under the Emergency Powers Act of 1920. That, it is to be hoped is highly improbable, but in the storm of political passions and of disturbed conditions, it is by no means inconceivable."

(Page 250)

The power of the Party Cabinet is now such that the same regulation which enabled it to imprison British subjects without trial and without suspending the Habeas Corpus Acts and avoiding an act of indemnity for doing so can be used against the membership of the House of Commons and has established as a matter of precedent a position which when Charles I attempted it led to the outbreak of the Civil Wars, namely to imprison any member of the House of Commons without trial and without disclosing to the House the reasons for such imprisonment.

Captain Maule Ramsey, member for Midlothian and Peebles was kept in prison under Regulation 18B for over four years with no trial or any disclosure of the reason for his imprisonment. He was not expelled from the House of Commons and whilst in prison, though subject to normal prison discipline and restrictions, was sent all his Parliamentary papers but which he was for long periods not permitted to examine. When Captain Ramsay appealed to the Committee of Privileges, a general doctrine was propounded that it is now legitimate for the executive to have such powers. This was given in the Report of the Committee and accepted by the House of Commons, and it read:-

> "In the struggle of Parliament against the Crown privilege was regarded as a protection of the Member of Parliament against the executive authority not responsible to Parliament. Thus Blackstone stated that 'privilege of Parliament was principally established in order to protect its Members not only from being molested by their fellow subjects, but also more especially from being oppressed by the power of the Crown'. This aspect of the question was emphasised by Captain Ramsey in the representation which he made before your Committee. The fact that the Executive is now responsible to Parliament and that powers such as those in question in this case can only be exercised if conferred by Parliament itself, is relevant when considering general statements such as that quoted from Blackstone, made at the time of or in relation to the conflict."

(No. 164, 8th October, 1940)

The Committee of Privileges reported its conclusion which was accepted by the House of Commons that:-

> "Preventative arrest under statutory authority by executive order is not within the principle of the cases to which the privilege from arrest has been decided to extend. To claim that the privilege extends to such cases would be either the assertion of a new Parliamentary privilege or an unjustified extension of an existing one. No question of any infringement of the privilege of freedom of speech arises."

Thus, a party Government controlling the majority membership of the House of Commons is now able to obtain statutory authority to arrest and imprison any Member of Parliament for an indefinite period without a trial and without disclosing the reason for such imprisonment, either at the time of the imprisonment or at any subsequent time.

This is now an established constitutional position not limited to wartime conditions but can be cited for similar action at any time. As long as this doctrine stands unrepudiated by the House of Commons, there can be no independent House of Commons, and without an independent House of Commons there can be no protection of the constitutional rights and liberties of the free-born British person.

The Courts now can do little to preserve the free system of English law or protect constitutional rights. They either have their powers removed into other hands, or they are tied by legislation by which the Party Cabinet expresses its now sovereign will.

Professor G.W. Keeton in his "Elementary Principles of Jurisprudence", writes;-

> "In England there has been a notable abdication of sovereign functions by Parliament in favour of the Executive in the present century evidenced by...the steady withdrawal of important classes of disputes from the jurisdiction of the ordinary courts and their transfer to administrative tribunals. Side by side with this, there has developed an increasing rigid party

system which has progressively deprived the private member of power and has placed him increasingly within the control of the Executive."

(2nd. edit., p. 60)

Professor C. J. Hamson, Reader in Comparative law at Cambridge, in his broadcast address in October, 1952 on "The Present Condition of the Law", said:-

> "Since the power so given to Parliament is utterly arbitrary, the judges strove, in the abstract very reasonably, to restrain it by process of interpretation. This process in turn led to our astonishing method of drafting statutes, with a meticulous particularity which to a continental lawyer seems incomprehensible. Upon pain of saying nothing, Parliament was compelled to say what it meant to a degree which is almost self stultifying. And this method of drafting which incidentally makes Parliamentary debate more difficult, further confirmed the judges in their view that from an act of Parliament or from regulations made there under neither rhyme nor reason is to be expected."

(Law Reform and Law Making, Heffers, 1953, p.2.)

The late Lord MacMillan in 1948 declared:-

> "The lover of our ancient laws and institutions which we have inherited from our fathers cannot but look on with some dismay at the process which we see daily in operation around us whereby the ancient and customary law of the land which has served us so well in the past, is being more and more superseded by a system of laws which have no regard for the usages and customs of the people, but are dictated by ideological theories. There will soon be little of our Common Law left either in England or in Scotland and the Statutory Rules and Orders will take its place. The work of our Courts is

more and more concerned with the interpretation of
often unintelligible legislation and less concerned with
the discussion and development of legal principles."

(The Times, 6th April, 1948)

These Statutory Rules and Orders now flooding our legal system have
no constitutional validity. They are only accepted as law by Austinian
doctrine. C. H. S. Fifoot, in his "English Law and its Background", points
out:-

"Subordinate legislation is now a major factor in the
life of the ordinary citizen. The Statute Book formidable
as it is, is slender in comparison with the mass of rules
and orders issued under the authority of some Act of
Parliament. The phenomenon is not difficult to explain.
A simple conception of government as the means of
securing order and independence allowed the language
of Austinian sovereignty to be applied to the problem of
constitutional law."

(Page 190)

No less disturbing is the setting up of independent courts, the so-
called administrative tribunals. Their purpose is to ensure that the will
of the Party Cabinet Executive prevails, and they have a procedure totally
incompatible with English legal procedure. These courts are expressly
designed to defeat the rule of law as established by the Statute of
Northampton, in which it was enacted that the law shall be administered
regardless of the command of the government. It is significant that these
tribunals follow the same principles of the courts in Roman Civil Law
communities where they are outside Common Law influence. They have
no "day in court", no jury, nor are decisions determined by precedent. The
judges are civil servants, and decisions are based not on the reasoned
judgement of the hearing official. The argument that such courts serve
only particular purposes is completely specious.

Coke lists over fifty different courts in his day, each with a procedure of
their own and most of them specialists in their own jurisdiction. But they
were all subject to the provision of Northampton. The purpose of these
modern administrative tribunals is to enforce the will of the government,

regardless of justice and right, and without any reference to the consent of the people.

Today we have the consequences of the "Law Reform" which the Benthamites carried through. The nature of these reforms, which aimed at the establishment of a parliamentary democratic despotism, can be judged by the fact that they were inspired by lord Mansfield when he aimed to establish a parliamentary royal despotism in the early years of the reign of George III.

In his "Law and Opinion in England", Dicey tells us:-

> "Two reformers arose of equal though of different genius. The one was Lord Mansfield, the other Bentham...Lord Mansfield as Chief Justice of England presided over the King's Bench for twenty-four years; he was not only in name but in reality, the head of the English Common Law. He was a jurist of genius, he filled a position of unrivalled authority; he achieved as much in the name of reform as was achievable by the means at his disposition. Yet his labours taken as a whole were not crowned with success...Bentham learnt the lesson of Lord Mansfield's career...he determined or assumed that the law must be reformed if at all by Parliamentary enactment."
>
> (Page 165)

But what are the facts?

Mansfield though an English judge, was, in fact, a Roman Civilian lawyer. According to his fellow countryman and admirer, Lord Campbell, Mansfield maintained that the foundation of jurisprudence was the Roman Civil Law. (Lives of the Chief Justices of England, Vol. III, p.186) He further said that:-

> "He did not sufficiently appreciate the merits of the old Common Law, overlooking the love of public liberty displayed by many of its maxims."
>
> (Ibid. p. 187)

This he reinforced by saying:-

> "He found a very low estimate of the Common Law of
> England which he was to administer."

(Ibid. P. 274)

The outstanding failure of Lord Mansfield's career as Lord Chief
Justice of England was his attempts to reform the law of England along
the very lines of accommodation to the despotic tenets of the Roman Civil
Law, which English law had so successfully resisted in the past centuries.

The true character of Mansfield's attempt to reform English law can
be judged from the words of C. H. S. Fifoot, who is clearly an admirer,
in his work "Lord Mansfield", where he tells us that the English legal
practitioners:-

> "suspected that behind the facade of precedent which
> he assumed to venerate, strange experiments were
> in progress and that, like the Prerogative Lawyers of
> the previous century, he sought to employ orthodox
> weapons in a sinister cause. The suspicion was not
> without a colour of truth. Lord Mansfield, if he was
> abreast of contemporary technique, was in advance
> of contemporary thought. Too rational to appreciate
> the affectionate care with which Fearne cultivated his
> feudal heritage, too penetrating to accept as an ultimate
> solution Blackstone's superficial reconciliation of
> medieval doctrine and modern society, he strained a
> legal faith to the verge of heresy."

(Page 229)

Mansfield's constitutional views can be gathered from the letter of
November 14th 1770, addressed as if to him by Junius, in which he wrote:-

> "I see through your whole life one uniform plan to
> enlarge the power of the crown at the expense of the
> liberty of the subject. To this object your thoughts,
> words, and actions have been constantly directed. In
> contempt or ignorance of the Common Law of England,

you have made it your study to introduce into the court where you preside maxims of jurisprudence unknown to Englishmen.

The Roman Code, the law of nations, and opinion of foreign civilians are your perpetual theme; but who ever heard you mention Magna Carta or the Bill of Rights with approbation of respect? By such treacherous arts the noble simplicity and free spirit of our Saxon laws were first corrupted...It is remarkable enough, but I hope not ominous, that the laws you understand best, and the judges you affect to admire most, flourished in the decline of a great empire, and are supposed to have contributed to its downfall."

The figure of Mansfield is hidden in a mysterious obscurity, but that he played the most decisive part in the events of his time, cannot be overlooked. According to Lord Campbell, (Lives of the Chief Justices of England), there was no one for fifteen years who more influenced the counsels of the nation, both at home and abroad.

This assessment received further support in the "Cambridge Modern History", where it is recorded that, by 1770:-

"The real direction of affairs was being assumed by the King, whose most confidential advisers were Mansfield and Sir Gilbert Elliot, the Treasurer of the Navy."

(Vol. 6, p. 442)

Dealing with the American unrest which led to the American Revolution, the same authorities state:-

"The government turned a deaf ear to the petition of Congress, the last presented by William Penn being contemptuously dismissed, largely it would seem, through the influence of Mansfield."

How little note has been taken of lord Mansfield's part in the early years of George III's reign can be seen in the fact that his name does not appear in the index in Dr. Herbert Butterfield's penetrating examination of this period in his work "George III and the Historians". He has, however, one reference to him on Page 263, where he quotes from Horace Walpole's "Memoirs of the Reign of George III":-

> "The Cabinet was so framed to enchance bold and arbitrary measures and Lord Mansfield who was always ready to suggest them, retained great weight in the Government."

Mansfield was a member of the Cabinet Council in successive and different administrations, and it can hardly be doubted that his views on constitutional issues must have carried great weight, and must, on many occasions, have proved decisive. In his "The Political History of England 1760- 1801", William Hunt recalls that Mansfield, even in his seventy-sixth year, "retained his mastery of constitutional law..." (Vol. 10, p. 207)

The constitutional situation was governed by the Regency Act of 1705, which repealed the Place Clause of the Act of Settlement of 1701, by which no one in receipt of any form of patronage from the Crown could be a member of the House of Commons. The repeal of this clause made it possible for George III to use his prerogative in the appointments to office and honour to influence the majority of the members of the House of Commons to give blind support to his Ministers who acted under his direct command.

Under the guidance of Mansfield, a claim to Parliamentary pre-eminence was put forward, which had never been suggested before. Parliament had only in the previous decade acknowledged that its authority, though supreme, rested on the consent of the people. In obedience to popular clamour, Parliament, in 1753, repealed an Act it had itself passed only in the previous Session. On that occasion, Hardwicke, then Lord Chancellor, declared:-

> "If the Act were of much greater importance than it is, I should be for repealing it; for however much the people may be misled, yet in a free country, I do not think an unpopular measure ought to be obstinately persisted in."
>
> (Parliamentary History of England (Hansard) Vol. XV, Col.102)

Under Lord Mansfield's new doctrine, it was claimed that an absolute obedience must be accorded to Parliament, and that this must in no case whatever be questioned, much less resisted, by the people. The people had the sole duty of passive obedience. Lord Mansfield was now claiming that:-

> "When the supreme power abdicates, the government is dissolved."

(Ibid. Col. 176, Vol. XVI)

This being the case, every means of coercion is justified to enforce authority. It was, however, clear that this new pre-eminence of sovereignty of Parliament was propounded not to enhance the independent authority of Parliament but solely to enhance the authority of the statesmen appointed by the King and dependent solely on the King's will.

It was this constitutional development which at home led to the crisis associated with John Wilkes and the Middlesex elections and which led to the American revolution abroad.

Burke pointed out to the legal right of the English people to resist. In "Present Discontents", he declared:-

> "In the situation in which we stand, with an immense revenue, an enormous debt, mighty establishments, Government itself a great banker and a great merchant, I see no other way for a decent attention to public interest in the representatives *but the interposition of the body of the people itself,* whenever it should appear by some flagrant or notorious act, by some capital innovation, that these representatives are going to overlap the fences of the law and introduce an arbitrary power. This interposition is a most unpleasant remedy but if it be a legal remedy, it is intended on some occasion to be used then only when it is evident that nothing else can hold the Constitution to its true principles."

(Burke's italics) (World Classics LXXXI, Vol. 12, p. 74)

It was this right of resistance by the people, confirmed by the English Revolution of !688, on which the Americans relied, and it was on these rights that they established their own democracy. Mansfield must be regarded as the precursor of Austinian Jurisprudence on which Dicey based his doctrine of Parliamentary sovereignty under which the English people have lost their historic constitutional rights and liberties and their consent is no longer the basis of Law in England.

For a thousand years, the English people have clung to their conception of law as derived from their own consent, and they have shown it to be not only practical but to have produced the most stable and enduring system of government under which this small people, inhabiting half an island grew to be the most powerful influence in the development of all that is best in western civilisation. What is no less remarkable is that English law has been recognised as one of the greatest systems of jurisprudence in the world today, unequalled by any other concept except that of the Roman people.

It is no coincidence but an identification of the greatest significance that both Roman and English Law are fundamentally similar in their conception of law, though developed independently of each other and the English even in antagonism to the tenets of the Roman code. Each was developed by the juristic process on fundamental principles which enshrined the national aspirations, that of Rome in the Law of the Twelve Tables and that of England symbolised by Magna Carta. Both great systems recognised the source of authority in the consent of the people as the product of reason, and by this means, established similar principles as the basis of their magnificent and enduring systems. As Buckland and McNair point out in their introduction to their work "Roman Law and Common Law":-

> "There is more affinity between the Roman jurist and
> the Common Lawyer than there is between the Roman
> jurist and his modern civilian successors."

(Page XI)

And as Lord Bryce has pointed out in his "Studies in History and Jurisprudence":-

> "England has applied more successfully than the
> Romans did the conception of the rights of the citizen

as against the organs of the state, but the conception is fundamentally Roman."

(Vol. 13 p. 192)

In this common approach to law lies the secret of national destiny and of civilisation itself. It is the major tragedy of the West that since the Renaissance it was the corruption of Roman Law which was received as the great jurisprudence of the Roman people. It is no less significant that today, in this period of decline, English jurisprudence, having abandoned the juristic principles of her Common Law, follows the tenets of the corrupted jurisprudence of the declining Roman imperialism.

THE SUPREMACY OF PARLIAMENT AND THE RULE OF LAW

In his introduction to the ninth (1939) edition of Dicey's "Law of the Constitution", Professor Wade remarked:-

> "The habitual exercise of supreme legislative authority by one power...the Parliament of the United Kingdom - which in its turn is more and more subordinated to the will of the administration, or Executive Government, for the time being suggests that this legal supremacy is capable of use to effect changes of a revolutionary character by those whom the electorate have placed in power. In particular, it appears, that the advent by constitutional means of the Totalitarian State can be more readily achieved by a Parliament which has power to destroy as well as to create the whole framework of Government by a simple act or series of acts. It is obvious that if a majority in the House of Commons can do what it likes with our liberties, we should be safer with a written constitution."

(Page LVI)

The proposal of a written constitution may indeed pose the constitutional problem that faces us but it cannot solve it. No written instrument has preserved a free constitution in communities whose legal systems are basically despotic. France has not yet found democratic stability with her fifteen written constitutions since her first revolution in the eighteenth century. The Nazi Party dictatorship was "constitutionally" established within the written provisions of the Weimar Republic of Germany, considered to be the most perfect democratic instrument ever devised. The proposal of a written constitution is no doubt inspired by American example, but American stability arises from the same causes which gave England her past stability without a written constitution. Today the proposal of a written constitution for England can only raise far more problems than it can solve. Who is going to write up such a constitution? On what principles can national agreement be achieved? Even if such a written constitution could be devised, what degree of permanency can it have? There is in England only one means whereby such a written constitution could be enacted and that is by act of Parliament. No act of Parliament can be given an immutable quality as Parliament cannot restrict its own supremacy, nor the supremacy of its successors. An act of Parliament has therefore, no permanent quality which a subsequent totalitarian party majority may not destroy. It is only necessary in a moment of high emotion for such a clique to gain a majority control of a subsequent House of Commons, and this protection could be swept away.

Even more perplexing is how such a written constitution would differ from the constitutional enactments of the past. Our constitution is embedded in written charters, declarations and statutes of the most solemn and almost sacred nature. These have never been repealed or repudiated, but they have ceased to have any validity. What possible steps can be taken to ensure that a newly written constitution is preserved from sharing the same fate?

The root of our problem does not lie in the absence of a written constitution but lies in the total nullification of all constitutional law, and the only purpose of a written constitution is to restore some legal basis to our form of government. But if a doctrine of Parliamentary sovereignty is to remain, then a written constitution is altogether without any meaning. If, on the other hand, the proposal of a written constitution is intended to modify or mitigate the consequences of the doctrine of Parliamentary sovereignty, then it must be clearly recognised that such an intention means the outright rejection of this doctrine. Austinian sovereignty is absolute and cannot be modified or mitigated. The proposal of a written constitution must therefore be taken as an admission that the doctrine of Austinian sovereignty as applied to Parliament is false. In other words, the law of our Parliamentary constitution has always been and still is valid and in full force and any departure from it by constitutional convention, which the doctrine of Parliamentary sovereignty allowed, is invalid and illegal. In England today, therefore, we need no paper constitution. We still have one in the greatest constitution of government the world has ever seen, not only established in law, but what is more, established in the hearts and souls of the English people. It represents no new fangled concoction of intellectual activity, but it enshrines centuries of hard practical experience, the records of which are part of our history, and its institutions are still part of our everyday national existence.

The restoration of the rule of law in England is now the decisive issue which faces British people. In Halsbury's "Laws of England", in the section on Constitutional Law, we are given the definition of the Rule of Law, which reads:-

> "From the all pervading presence of law as the sole source of governmental powers and duties there follow these consequences.
>
> The existence or non-existence of a power or duty is a matter of law and not of fact and so must be determined by reference to some enactment or reported case. The fact of a continued undisputed exercise of a power is immaterial unless it points to a customary power exercised from time immemorial. In particular, the existence of a power cannot be proved by the practice of a private office.
>
> (2nd edit., Vol. 6.)

The authority now exercised by the Party Cabinet system does not conform to this definition of the Rule of Law in that the Cabinet does not exercise a customary power from time immemorial, nor has it a legislative foundation. The same consideration applies to the doctrine of Parliamentary sovereignty. Parliament today still legislates in the form of advice and consent to the enactments of the King's most excellent majesty. Thus Parliament still recognises that it is on the wearer of the English Crown that the rule of law depends and that legal sovereignty lies there and nowhere else. The King, and only the King, represents the eminent domain of the nation.

As Burke pointed out in his speech on May 30th, 1794:-

> "The Sovereignty of Great Britain is in the King, he is the sovereign of the Lords and the sovereign of the

Commons individually and collectively; and as he has his prerogative established by law, he must exercise it and all persons claiming and deriving under him whether by Act of Parliament, whether by Charter of the Crown, or by any other mode whatsoever, all are alike, bound by law and responsible to it. No one can assume or receive any power of sovereignty because this sovereignty is in the Crown and cannot be delegated away from the Crown."

(Works of Edmund Burke, Bohn's British Classics, 1857, Vol. VIII, p. 7)

But whereas the doctrine of Parliamentary sovereignty postulates that Parliament stands above the law, including the constitution of Parliament itself, and thus nullifies all constitutional law, the sovereignty of the King of England is under God and the law and establishes the English King as the supreme guardian of English law as derived from the consent of the people on which their constitutional rights and liberties depend.

In Halsbury's "Laws of England", in the section headed "Constitutional Law", it is further recorded that:-

"The prerogative is thus created and limited by Common Law and the sovereign can claim no prerogative except such as the law allows nor such as are contrary to Magna Carta or any other Statute or to the liberty of the subject. The courts have jurisdiction therefore to enquire into the existence or extent of any alleged prerogative, it being a maxim of the Common Law that *Rex non debet esse sub homine, sed sub Deo et Lege quia lex facit regem*. If any prerogative is disputed, they must decide the question whether or not it exists in the same way as they decide any other question of law. If a prerogative is clearly established, they must take note of it like any other rule of law."

For this reason, it is fundamental to the English Constitution that the royal prerogative being vested in the Crown by Law, the Crown cannot part with it except by parliamentary legislation. In the 1932 edition of Halsbury's "Laws of England", it is laid down that:-

> "The general rule is that the prerogative cannot be affected or parted with by the Crown except by express statutory authority."

Today by a process other than statutory, the prerogative of the Crown has been alienated from the Crown. As Sir Lewis Namier has shown in his Romanes Lecture of 1952:-

> "The Prime Minister replaced the Sovereign as actual head of the Executive when the choice of the Prime Minister no longer lay with the Sovereign; the Sovereign lost the choice when strongly organised and disciplined parties came into existence; party discipline depends primarily on the degree to which the member depends on the party for his seat."

> (Personalities and Power, 1955, p. 14)

Under the modern doctrine of Parliamentary sovereignty by which all constitutional law is nullified, this position is covered by the Constitutional Conventions. As Sir Ivor Jennings, in his "Law and the Constitution", points out when writing on party action:-

> "One of the earliest results was the powers which are legally exercised by the King - the Royal Prerogative - were in practice exercised by the Cabinet. The King acted on the 'advice' of the Cabinet Ministers and in practice he could not refuse to take that advice unless he could find another set of Ministers who could keep a majority of the House of Commons. Hence there was by constitutional convention a transference of the Royal Prerogative to the Cabinet."

> (The Law and the Constitution, Ivor Jennings, 2nd edit p.86)

In place of the King ruling under God and the Law, we now have the Party leader under the name of Prime minister.

The Prime Minister is not elected by the people or even by the membership of his party. His appointment is the result of the party action of which the people in general and the members of the party, in particular, have little knowledge and over which they have no control. The office of Prime Minister is unknown to the constitution, and in accepting office, the party leader undergoes no inaugural service. As Professor Ramsey Muir remarks in "How England is Governed":-

> "He (the Prime Minister) is, in fact, though not in law, the working head of the State, endued with such a plenitude of power as no other constitutional ruler in the world possesses, not even the President of the United States... The whole strength of the Prime Minister rests upon the fact that he is Party Chief, the recognised leader of a party which has obtained a majority, or at least a larger number of seats than any other party, in the House of Commons, whether it has the support of the majority in the nation or not."

(How Britain is Governed, Ramsey Muir, p.83)

Sir John Marriot, in his "English Political Institutions", pointed out that the British Prime Minister, when supported by a stable and substantial majority in Parliament, has greater power than the former German Emperors or the American President. The reach of these powers is such:-

> "(that)...he can alter the laws, he can impose taxation and repeal it, and he can direct all the forces of the State.

> (English Political Institutions, J. A. R. Marriot, Oxford 1910. P. 89)

H. R. G. Greaves, in his "British Constitution", asserts that:-

> "The Prime Minister is far the most powerful man in the country. He is sometimes and not without reason likened to a dictator. His formal powers at least, resemble closely to those of an autocrat. The prerogatives lost by the Monarch have fallen for the most part into his hands, as chief responsible advisor to the Crown. Those which have not been inherited by him direct have gone to the

Cabinet; but he is the leading member; he forms it; he can alter it or destroy it. The Government is the master of the country and he is the master of the Government... Nor is it primarily because his powers are exercised differently that the Prime Minister's position is unlike that of a dictator. Both are leaders of a party holding certain philosophy, with certain principles. Both must consult advisers and interests before they act, if their action is to prove generally acceptable. Both are bound to consider consequences and cannot act merely arbitrarily as the whim takes them."

(The British Constitution, H. R. G. Greaves, Allen Unwin 1938 p. 108)

The King is now totally eliminated from the operation of our modern political system.

Only once in our whole history has English Kingship ceased to operate, and that was three centuries ago on the outbreak of the Civil Wars. Then for the first time, English Government was without the legal authority of a king, and in consequence, the whole period till the restoration in 1660 is a legal void and the authority of Parliament in that period has never been recognised.

Denzil Holles, one of the leading parliamentary opponents to Charles I and one of the five members of the House of Commons whom Charles attempted to arrest, has in his memoirs left his estimate of the nature of that lawless rule when he wrote:-

"The meanest of men, the basest and vilest of the nation, the lowest of the people have got the power into their hands; trampled upon the Crown; baffled and misused Parliament, violated the laws; destroyed or suppressed the liberties of the people in general; broke asunder all bonds and ties of religion, conscience, duty, loyalty, faith, common honesty and good manners; cast off all fear of God and man and now Lord it over the persons and estates of all sorts and ranks from the King on his throne to the beggar in his cottage; making their will their law; their hair-brained, giddy fanatical humour the end of all their actions."

Following the execution of Charles I, the monarchy was eliminated not only in fact but in theory and supreme authority, vested in a Committee of Parliament known as "The Keepers of the Liberty of England by authority of Parliament". This failed and led to the Protectorate of Oliver Cromwell, confirmed by a written constitution known as "The Instrument of Government". Despite the strength and statesmanship of Cromwell, there was no settlement. To achieve this, only one solution presented itself, namely, the restoration of the Crown to full constitutional authority. This solution was not only that of the Royalist party, it was the solution of the Republicans themselves. The very men who had taken an active part in destroying kingship on principle, now sought the restoration of royal government. The protectorate Parliament, acting under the Instrument of Government, prepared a humble petition and advice and sent a large deputation to Lord Protector Cromwell to urge him to assume the title of King. This was a constitutional move and no act of flattery, as can be seen from the arguments used by the members of the deputation. The following extracts must suffice as to weighty conclusions that the republicans reached on English kingship.

William Lenthall, the famous speaker of the Long Parliament and of the inter-regnum Parliament of 1653 and Master of the Rolls in the Commonwealth, was a member of this deputation. Speaking to the title of King, Lenthall said:-

> "For upon due consideration you will find that the whole body of the law is carried upon this wheel, it is not a thing that stands on the top merely, but runs through the whole life and veins of the law...The grounds and reason why they (the people) have adhered to this title (of King) was for the maintenance of their liberties... you now have a title (of Lord Protector) that may extend where it will, it hath no limit at all...you have no limit by any rule of law that I understand."
>
> (The Parliamentary or Constitutional History, Vol. 21, p. 73)

Sir John Glynne, Chief Justice of the Upper Bench in the Commonwealth, another member of the Parliamentary deputation said:-

> "The name of King is a name known by law...and these are the grounds why the Parliament make it their request that your Highness would assume that title. If so be your Highness should do any act and one should come and say "My Lord Protector you are sworn to govern by Law and yet you do thus and thus as lord Protector, why the king could not have done so. 'Aye' say you 'but I am not King. I am not bound to do as the King; I am lord Protector, shew me that the law doth require me to do it as Protector... Why you put anyone in a stumble in that case...The king's prerogative is known by law...is under the Courts of Justice and is bound as well as any acre of land or anything that a man hath."

> (Ibid. p. 78)

Another member of this great deputation was Sir Charles Wolsely, a member of Cromwell's Council of State, who said:-

> "The reason why things of late have been so unsettled hath been because there hath been no legal head... This nation has ever been a lover of monarchy and of monarchy under the title of King. The name and office for above a thousand years have been in this nation. 'Tis the Great Common Law that is the custom of the nation, approved for good by many ages, to have the office and the name of a King. No new law that makes any other can have that validity which the custom of so many ages back hath...I hope then, Sir, that you will give the people leave to name their own servant."

> (The Parliamentary or Constitutional History, Vol. 21, p. 73)

John Lisle, the regicide, had this to say:-

> "National justice does consist of two things; that you do right to the people with respect to their just privileges

in relation to the Parliament; that you do right to the people in respect to their just rights according to the law of the land. Sir, the nation's rights in Parliament can never be done to the people unless Parliament hath its ancient rights in relation to the Government. And they can never have their right in relation to the law unless the laws have their ancient right in relation to the Government.

Sir, the remonstrance offered to your Highness is the covenant of the three nations, both for spiritual and civil liberties. If there was a proper time to make David king when they covenanted with him at Hebron, it is now a proper time for you to accept this title when the Parliament hath brought this with a covenant for the three nations that relates to their civil and spiritual liberties."

(The Parliamentary or Constitutional History, Vol. 21, p. 85)

Had Cromwell accepted the title, he could have been legal King of England in the same way as the attained Henry Tudor became Henry VII after the Battle of Bosworth. However, under the influence of the army, he refused a title which would have limited his powers.

Following the experience of Cromwellian dictatorship, Parliament took action to ensure the position of the Crown in the most emphatic positive legislation, which is not repealed by enacting that: -

"...By the undoubted and fundamental laws of this kingdom, neither the peers of the realm nor the Commons, nor both together in Parliament or out of Parliament, nor the people collectively or representatively nor any other persons whatsoever had, hath, have or ought to have any coercive power over the persons of the Kings of this realm."

(The Statutes Revised, 2nd edit., Vol. 1, Chas. II, c. 30, 1660, p. 609)

By another unrepealed Act of Parliament it is further enacted:-

> "If any person or persons at any time...shall maliciously
> and advisedly by writing, printing or preaching or other
> speaking express , publish, utter, declare or affirm that
> both Houses or either House of Parliament have or hath
> legislative power without the King, or any other words
> to the same effect, such persons so foresaid offending
> shall occur the danger and penalty of a praemunire."

(Ibid. Chas. II, C. I., S. 3., 1661, p. 613)

The penalties of praemunire are the most serious short of being capital.

Nevertheless, Walter Bagehot, in the "English Constitution", so highly commended by Dicey and still accepted as a guide, was able to lay down the new constitutional doctrine which as the Conventions of the Constitution Dicey would include as law:-

> "The popular theory of the English Constitution involves
> two errors as to the Sovereign.
>
> First, in its closest form at least, it considers him as an
> "Estate of the Realm" a separate co-ordinate authority
> with the House of Lords and the House of Commons.
> This and much else the Sovereign once was, but this
> he is no longer. That authority could only be exercised
> by a monarch with a legislative veto. He should be able
> to reject bills, if not as the House of Commons rejects,
> but at least as the House of Peers rejects them. But the
> Queen has no such veto. She must sign her own death
> warrant if the two Houses unanimously send it up to
> her. It is a fiction of the past to ascribe to her legislative
> power. She has now ceased to have any. Secondly the
> present theory holds that the Queen is the head of
> the Executive."

(The English Constitution, Walter Bagehot, World
Classics, CCCXXX, p. 51)

When law becomes fiction, and modern practice becomes authority, we have a measure indeed of the lawlessness of the modern political system.

Today with our greater experience of modern totalitarian party dictatorship, we may fully understand the admonition of Burke when he declared:-

> "We are members of a free country, and surely we all know that the machine of a free constitution is no simple thing; but is as intricate and delicate as it is valuable. We are members of a great and ancient monarchy and we must preserve religiously the true legal rights of the Sovereign which form the keystone that binds together the noble and well constructed arch of our Empire and our Constitution."
>
> (The Works of Edmund Burke, World Classics, LXXI, Vol. 2, p.166)

In the English Constitution, there can be no doctrine of a divine right of Kings nor of an indefeasible hereditary right in the wearer of the Crown. Both these doctrines of kingship arise from the conditions created by the Lex Regia of the revived Roman Law. The theory of a divine right of kings was propounded in answer to the claim of sovereignty, which the Canon Law as a derivative of the Roman Civil Law vested in the supreme head of the Catholic Church, a claim which England had resisted long before the Reformation. The doctrine of indefeasible hereditary right was the only means open in Civil Law communities to provide some remedy to the disturbance which would follow on the death of a sovereign when others might establish a claim to sovereign power by force of arms.

Never at any time in English history has a claim to divine right or indefeasible hereditary right been allowed to an English Monarch. Such a claim was put forward by Richard II, and he was deposed. It was not put forward again till the Scottish Kings came to the English throne. James I, was the first who seriously propounded this claim and there followed a century of constitutional struggle to deny its validity. If there is any doubt on this point, it is only necessary to turn to Rapin's *History of England*, (Volume 8, 4th edition, page 118) to see how emphatically he deals with this claim of James I. Writing in the eighteenth century before the party system had chosen to cloud the issue, he wrote:-

> "In the first place, no law can be produced on which may be founded the hereditary succession of the crown of England. Secondly, there are many precedents in English history which show that Parliament assumed a power to dispose of the crown, and settle the succession without any regard to the next heir. In the third place, more kings, since the Conquest, have mounted the throne by virtue of acts of Parliament, or some other means, than by hereditary rights. The first four especially, namely, William the Conqueror, William Rufus, Henry I and Stephen, most certainly came not to the crown by this right. When was it that the crown became hereditary?...In the fourth place, of all the kings from William the Conqueror to James I there was not one who had less right to the crown than Henry VII before he was confirmed by Parliament. It was therefore from Parliament's confirmation, rather than from Henry Seventh's hereditary rights, that James I could derive his own title...So James I in resolving to establish this pretended hereditary right, was the first cause of the troubles which afflicted England and which are not yet ceased."

In England, the sovereignty of the king is derived solely from the authority of Parliament, and that it is established on a hereditary basis is an expedient the soundness of which experience has confirmed beyond any doubt whatsoever. In England, there can be no such thing as a King de jure who is not also King de facto. Once established with his Parliamentary title, the sovereignty of the King is unassailable.

Since the Restoration of 1660, English constitutional kingship has never been challenged or attacked, not even by the political democrats of the party system. If anything it has been extolled. For example, on the very day (April 3rd, 1872) on which Disraeli first publicly paraded his new militarised party organisation by which the constitutional position of the crown has been reduced to a cypher, he declared:-

> "Since the settlement of the Constitution now nearly two centuries ago, England has never experienced a revolution though there is no country in which there has been so continuous and such considerable change. How is this? Because the wisdom of your forefathers placed the prize of supreme power without the sphere of human passions, whatever the struggle of parties, whatever the strife of factions, whatever the excitement and exultation of the public mind, there has always been something in this country round which all classes and parties could rally, representing the majesty of the law, the administration of justice and involving at the same time, the security for every man's rights and the foundation of honour."

(Life of Benjamin Disraeli, G. E. Buckle, Vol. 5, p. 166)

To this monarchy, the English people have ever shown their allegiance. As William Cowper, the lawyer poet, expressed it in "The Task":-

> "We love the King, who loves the law, respects his bounds,
> And reigns content with them; him we serve,
> Freely and with delight, who leaves us free;
> But recollecting still he is a man,
> We trust him not too far. King though he be,
> And King of England too, he may be weak,
> And vain enough to be ambitious still,
> May exercise amiss his proper powers,
> Or covet more than free men choose to grant;
> Beyond that mark is treason. He is ours,
> To Administer, to guard, to adorn the State,
> But not to warp or change it. We are his,
> To serve him nobly in the common cause,
> True to the death but not to be his slaves."

Under the doctrine that the king can do no wrong, the only prerogative which the King can exercise in his personal capacity is the appointment to office and honour. The exercise of this personal prerogative of appointment to office is, however, subject to the condition that everyone so appointed must have skill and capacity for the office to which he is appointed otherwise, the appointment is void, whereas those appointed to offices of state and administration must command the confidence of the House of Commons. This confidence can be withdrawn at any time, in which case the King is required to make another appointment which commands the confidence of the House of Commons, who have the power to enforce their will by being the sole tax raising authority. The position of the King in the exercise of his personal prerogative of appointment to office is that in his high and exalted position, the King can have no other personal ambition than the welfare and honour of the nation. In his appointments to office, the king as an hereditary monarch is least likely to have entered into commitments which may warp or distort his judgement of the qualifications of those he appoints. As supreme head of government for life, the long term approach to national policy is possible. From his position in the very centre of affairs, he can seek out ability, integrity, capacity and experience among his subjects wherever it is to be found and command these services in the national interests. Government is a highly complex art, and in our modern age involves highly specialised knowledge and experience. The monarchy is in a position in a national setting with a full knowledge of facts to judge men and administration and from where personalities can be weighed in relation to post and offices.

The English Constitutional executive authority is the King's Privy Council which has a record which goes back into the furthest recess of our history. The Privy Council represents the supremacy of national authority in action and is, therefore, next to the king the most eminent of his Councils. Of the Council Board, Coke tells us:-

"This is the most noble, honourable and revered assembly of the King and his Privy Council in the king's Court or Palace: with this Council the King himself doth sit at his pleasure. These councillors like good sentinels and watchmen, consult of, and for the public good and the honour, defence and profit of the realm."

(4th Institute, Ch.2, p. 53)

Clarendon, in his history of his life, written after the Restoration of 1660 tells us that:-

> "By the Constitution of this Kingdom and the very laws and customs of the nation, as the Privy Council and every member of it is the King's sole choice and election of him to that trust, (for the greatest office of the State, though conferred likewise by the King himself doth not qualify the office to be of the Privy Council or to be present in it, before a new assignation that honour is bestowed on him and that he be sworn of the Council) so that the body of it is most sacred, and has the greatest authority in the government of the State, next the person of the King himself to whom all others powers are equally subject; and no King of England can so secure his own just prerogatives or preserve it from violation as by a strict defending and support the dignity of his Privy Council."

(History of the Rebellion, Oxford U. P. 1843, p. 1189)

Without the advice and consent of the Privy Council, no resolution of the Crown, whether as to foreign affairs, or the issue of orders or of any administrative instructions or any public acts, could be acted upon. The Privy Council is governed by formal procedure, and its decisions are a matter of record.

Before its authority was abused by the notions of Roman Civil Law kingship, which the Scottish kings introduced into England with "the tendency ...to introduce the Roman Civil Law into judicial practice", as Sir Almeric Fitzroy records in "The history of the Privy Council" (Page 119), the Privy Council of England had fully established itself as one of the greatest organs of executive government in the world and the leading factor in the growth and development of English pre-eminence. Lord Eustace Percy, in his Stanhope essay of 1907, entitled "The Privy Council under the Tudors", gives us a summary of what this great institution of constitutional government achieved. There is here the story he tells us:-

> "Of men who are not afraid of the responsibility laid upon them nor shrank from the power that was put into their

hands - men who were strong enough to be the leaders and the guide of the nation in its days of storm and stress - men, who whatever their faults or their shortcomings gave their whole lives and talents to the work they had begun and having laid their hands to the plough were never known to falter or turn back. Through the century of religious and political unrest these men held England in the hands of an iron discipline; they watched over her commerce; they provided for the defence of her shores; they reduced her lawless provinces from chaos to order and good government; they gave her poor a justice that was untainted by corruption; to them she owed her unity and her strength; and to them and the great organisation whose members they were, she can at least accord today the title of the strongest and most patriotic government she has ever known."

(Page 73)

Though now usurped by the Party Cabinet, the Privy Council is still in Law the executive authority of the English nation and is still vested with the same authority as in Tudor days.

Under the English Parliamentary constitution, the exercise of any public authority whatsoever is subject to law and thus involves a continuous criminal responsibility to the English nation in Parliament, assembled. Not a few powerful ministers of the Crown, not a few favourites of the King himself have stood lonely figures in Westminster in Westminster Hall to answer charges of high crimes and misdemeanours made against them on impeachment by the House of Commons, acting as the Grand Inquest of the nation.

In a Parliamentary report of the Committee of the House of Commons made on the 30th April, 1794, there is a paragraph which fully shows the meaning of responsibility to Parliament when it says:-

"...this House has chosen to proceed in the High Court of Parliament because the inferior courts are habituated with very few exceptions to try men for the abuse only of their individual and natural powers which can extend but a little way. Before them offences whether fraud or violence or both, are much the greater part, charged upon persons of mean and obscure condition. Those unhappy persons are so far from being supported by men of rank influence that the whole weight of the community is directed against them. In this case they are, in general, objects of protection as well as punishment...In the cause which your managers have in charge the circumstances are the very reverse of what happens in mere personal delinquency which come before the inferior courts. These courts have not before them persons who act, and who justify their acts by the nature of a despotical and arbitrary power. The abuses, stated in our impeachment, are not those of mere individual faculties but the abuse of civil and political authority. The offence is that of one who has carried with him in the perpetration of his crimes whether of violence or fraud the whole force of the state; who in the perpetration and concealment of offences has had the advantages of all the means and powers given to government for the detection and punishment of guilt and for the protection of the people..."

Here we have the very essence of the meaning of responsibility to Parliament by which every corruption of power was defeated and by which the rights and liberties of the people were preserved.

The fact that the Royal prerogative has never been successfully abused in our Parliamentary constitution and all corruption of power been avoided is due to the independence of the House of Commons acting as the watchdog for the people of England. To fulfil its great and supreme function, the independence of the House of Commons is a cardinal principle of our Parliamentary constitution. This independence is not only that arising from freedom of election but includes freedom from fear of punishment or favour of patronage, and this stands confirmed in the Bill of Rights and the Act of Settlement. Under the principles thus confirmed, no member of the House of Commons could be appointed to any office of state or administration and be in receipt of any emolument by grace and favour of the Crown. The absolute freedom and independence of the members of the House of Commons is, therefore, a supreme condition of a legally constituted House of Commons.

In the reign of Queen Elizabeth I, Coke described the quality of this independence of the member of Parliament as being that of an elephant in that:-

> "First he hath no gall. Secondly, that he is inflexible and cannot bow. Thirdly, that he is of ripe and perfect memory, which properties, as it is said, ought to be in every member of the great Council of Parliament. First to be without gall, that is without malice, rancour, heat and envy, every gallish inclination (if any were) should tend to do the good of the whole body, the Commonwealth. Secondly, that he be constant, inflexible and not be bowed or turned from the right, either for fear, reward or favour, nor in the judgement respect any person. Thirdly of a ripe memory that they remembering perils past, might prevent dangers to come."

> (4th inst., Ch. 1. The High Court of Parliament, p.3)

Burke pointed out in "Present Discontents":-

> "The virtue spirit and essence of a House of Commons consists in it being the express image of the feelings of the nation. It is not instituted to be a control *upon* the people, as of late it has been taught by a doctrine of most pernicious tendency. It was designed as a control *for* the people. Other institutions have been formed for the purpose of checking popular excesses, and they are, I apprehend fully adequate to their object. If not they ought to be made so.

> The House of Commons as it was never intended for the support of peace and subordination is miserably appointed for that service...a vigilant and jealous eye over executory and judicial magistracy, an anxious care for public money; an openness approaching towards facility, towards public complaint: these seem to be the true characteristics of a House of Commons ...

> But a House of Commons full of confidence when the
> nation is plunged in despair, in utmost harmony with
> ministers whom the people regard with the utmost
> abhorrence ...who in all disputes between the people
> and the administration presume against the people,
> who punish their disorders but refuse even to inquire
> into the provocations to them this is an unnatural, a
> monstrous state of things in this constitution. Such an
> assembly may be a great, wise awful senate; but it is not
> to any popular purpose a House of Commons."

Under the party system today, membership of the House of Commons is a primary condition of any appointment to executive government, to which loyalty to party is rewarded. Members of the House of Commons are thus no longer the independent representatives of the people but are, first and foremost, representatives of party, which alone can satisfy their personal ambitions. Fear of punishment and favour of patronage is now the dominant consideration in most members of the House of Commons.

With this corruption of the House of Commons by the Party Cabinet system, the second co-ordinate institution of Parliament, namely the House of Lords as the supreme court of English Law, is degraded and debased. This is shown by its vast swollen membership which has resulted from the abuse of the royal prerogative as the fountain of honour by the Party Cabinet. How the House of Lords is to be restored to its rightful honour and dignity requires the consideration of its present membership and no one else. If it is proposed to reduce its swollen membership, say by a process of election of peers to sit in Parliament on the same basis as the Scottish peers have been selected, then the concurrence of the King and the House of Commons may be required if legislative authority is thought to be needful, but this decision must rest with the present peers. Whatever the proposals for the reform of the House of Lords are proposed, its restoration as the supreme court of English Law is of primary importance.

In his Romanes Lecture of 1959, "From Precedent to Precedent", Lord Denning concluded with his great appeal when he said:-

> "I have shown how in times past the House of Lords (in
> the days when lay peer sat and voted) used to correct
> errors into which the House itself or its predecessors

had fallen and how it used to create new precedents so as to meet new situations. If the law is to develop and not to stagnate, the House must, I think, recapture this vital principle - the principle of growth. The House of Lords is more than another court of law. It is more than another court of appeal. It is the court of Parliament itself. It acts for the Queen as the fountain of justice in our land. It must of course correct errors that have been made by the courts below; but it should do more. It lays down or should lay down the fundamental principles of the law to govern the people; and whilst adhering firmly to those principles, it should over-rule particular precedents that it finds to be at variance therewith. Then only shall we be able to claim that "Freedom broadens down from precedent to precedent."

(From Precedent to Precedent, Lord Denning, Romanes Lecture, 1959. p.33)

The collapse of the House of Lords as the Supreme Court of English Law is probably one of the main factors in the decline and decay of our constitutional system. This collapse began in the rise of a partisan spirit in which the House of Lords lost its standing as a judicial institution. An additional factor was a claim by the House of Lords to an appellate jurisdiction outside the field of Common Law. The appeal from all courts of special jurisdiction, particularly those which were governed by the Roman Civil Law or the Canon Law, was to the King in Council. This principle was broken when in the teeth of opposition of the House of Commons, the House of Lords claimed a final jurisdiction from the courts of Equity with the result that the Lord Chancellor had to sit in appeals from its own judgements. The worst blow, however, to the judicial standing of the House of Lords came with the act of Union with Scotland when the House of Lords undertook appeals from the Court of Session which administered the Roman Civil Law in Scotland. This was, if not against the strict letter, but most certainly against the intention of the Treaty of Union, which prohibited any appeals from the Scottish courts to the English courts at Westminster. These courts, as well as the House of Lords, were not competent to act in any issue arising in Roman Law. It is said that when the Scottish appeals first came up before the House of Lords, not a word of Justinian could be found in the House of Lords library. In these cases, the English judges were unable to give any advice, and the Scottish judges were not available. The membership of the House of Lords was completely confused and bewildered by this strange jurisprudence, and it was difficult at times to obtain a quorum to hear a case. The result was that the work fell upon a small group of English Law Lords who floundered around for their conclusions, and the House of Lords as the supreme court virtually ceased to exist.

The House of Lords has never since recovered its standing as a judicial authority, but it did continue to act as a senate in legislation. In this capacity, it offered some resistance to the development of Party Government until it was virtually crushed by the Parliament Act of 1911.

Today sitting in the House of Lords and in its name but with the lay membership not present though not legally excluded, we have the Lords of Appeal acting as the Supreme Court. The Lords of Appeal are professional lawyers, and this has led to the position that the bench of judges are not now called on for guidance and assistance, and the judges now have little or no influence in decisive legal issues, though bound to accept the decisions of the Lords of Appeal as final.

The outstanding feature of this body of lawyers acting in the name of the House of Lords is that they do not constitute a court of pure Common Law as included among their number are Scottish lawyers trained in the Civil Law but who nevertheless act as the final court of appeal on English cases.

The fundamental cleavage which exists between Roman Law and English Law divides the Scottish Law from that of England so much that even after a hundred and fifty years of the closest political union with a common language and a common border, the two laws were complete strangers to each other. As Lord Justice Clerk Hope declared in the Court of Session in 1851:-

> "The more I am able to collect of English Law, I am only the more confident that we do not understand nine out of ten cases which are quoted to us and in attempting to apply that law, we run the greatest risk of spoiling our own by mis-understanding theirs."
>
> (Lord Justice Clerk Hope, M'Cowen v. Wright, 15 Dec., 1852)

If this is so, how can a Scottish judge be competent to act as a member of the supreme court of English Law? The difference is not just a technical one, but one that profoundly affects the juristic process. The Late Lord MacMillan, an eminent Scottish Lawyer, pondered greatly on the fundamental difference of the two legal systems when he himself became a Lord of Appeal. In his "Law and Other Things," he wrote:-

> "I was not long in discovering how entirely different are the historical backgrounds of the English and Scottish Law. I found myself encountering the fundamental distinction between the methods of the two greatest products of the human intellect which the world has ever seen, the Civil Law and the Common Law."

> (Law and Other Things, Lord MacMillan, Cambridge, U. P. 1938, Two Ways of Thinking, p. 78)

Lord MacMillan, can, however, hardly conceal the contempt which the civilian lawyer feels for our Common Law. He quotes with obvious approval, the words of its arch enemy when he wrote:-

> "The judges of England were said by Bentham to have made the Common Law as a man makes a law for his dog - by waiting till he has done something wrong and then beating him for it. Thus the law of England was a product of practitioners not of professors, of practical men, not philosophers."

> (Ibid., p. 80)

But Lord Macmillan nowhere showed appreciation of the outstanding fact that the Law of English practitioners laid the foundation of the most enduring and exalted system of free government in the history of civilisation whilst his professors and philosophers developed from Roman Law the legal foundations of the worst tyrannies and despotisms in our Western World. How can it be said that a Scottish Civilian is competent to adjudicate in the final court of Appeal in a case affecting the constitutional liberties of English subjects? In Scotland, the liberty of the subject is established by legislation which is revocable. In England, the liberty of the subject is fundamental and, therefore, an irrevocable condition in the exercise of all legal authority. No Civilian can appreciate this decisive distinction which arises between the two systems of law.

This Roman Law influence in our Supreme Court of Appeal is enhanced by the reception of Austinian jurisprudence and provoked one of our greatest Common Lawyers to protest in an issue closely affecting the liberty of the subject. Lord Aitkin speaking on the Liversidge v. Anderson judgement, declared:-

> "I view with apprehension the attitude of judges, who , on a mere question of construction, when face to face with claims involving the liberty of the subject, show themselves more executive minded than the executive. In England amidst the clash of arms, the laws are not silent. They may be changed, but they speak the same language in war as in peace. It has always been one of the pillars of freedom, one of the principles of liberty for which on recent authority we are now fighting, that the judges are no respecters of persons and stand between the subject and any attempted encroachments on his liberty by the executive, alert to see that any coercive action is justified in law. In this case I have listened to arguments which might have been addressed acceptably to the Court of King's bench in the time of Charles I."

> (All England Law Reports, 1941, Vol. 3, House of Lords, p. 361C)

As the supreme court, apart from any conflict of legal theory, this arrangement of the Lords of appeal sitting as the House of Lords set up by the Supreme Court of Judicature Acts in the seventies of the last century has proved a failure. Professor C. J. Hamson, Reader of Comparative Law in the University of Cambridge, pointed out in his broadcast talks in October, 1952, on the "Present Condition of the Law", that:-

> "It was the boast of English Law, that proceeding by experience from case to case and untrammelled by the rigid form of a code, it was capable of its own motion of dealing with the changing circumstances around it

and grew as a living thing having within itself its own power of development. Well, why does it not continue to be able to adapt itself today? It is all very well for the judges to claim that they are not responsible for the statute law, but for the case law, the law the judges made, surely the judges are responsible? In this specialised context, when I say 'judges' I mean more particularly the House of Lords (i.e. Lords of Appeal) in their capacity of supreme tribunal in the land; for they may prima facie be regarded as the natural form for the redress of our case law."

(Law Reform and Law Making, C. J. Hamson, Heffer, 1953, p. 4)

Professor Hampson, in developing his theme, declared that:-

"It seems to be agreed by everyone including the House of Lords (i. e. Lords of appeal) that as things are now, what is required is not an appeal *to* the House, but an appeal *from* the House."

(ibid)

And then he proceeds:-

"It is certainly to be observed that the House does adopt today towards case law that curious attitude which is regarded as appropriate to Statute Law- an attitude as I would describe it, of carefully cultivated irresponsibility. We do find the House saying, as regards case law also 'That is the law'. We agree that it is silly or unfortunate. We cannot help it. If you dislike it go to Parliament'... It is this claim of present irresponsibility for the state of our case law by the House of Lords which I would specify as the fundamental cause of the disease of our law. Among supreme tribunals, the House is, I believe, singular in making such a claim. In this matter it presents a contrast, much to its own disadvantage, with the United States Supreme Court. If that Court had adopted as regards the American Constitution the attitude which the House adopted towards the Common Law, the United States would long ago have been reduced to chaos..."

(ibid. p. 7)

If we bear in mind that every member of the House of Lords above the age of 21 is still today a judge of English law with a standing equal to any judge in the Courts of Law and not inferior to the Lord Chancellor, the Lord Chief Justice or any other of the Lords of Appeal, it should be a matter for consideration of the present membership of the House of Lords as to whether they can allow the continuance in their name and with their tacit consent of such a situation. Whatever the reasons, the Supreme Court of judicature Acts perpetuated the lay membership of the House of Lords as the supreme court. Those Acts were passed with the consent of the House of Lords so that the lay members still constitute the High Court of Parliament with a right to sit and vote in all judgement given in the name of their House. This right imposes a responsibility. Whatever now proceeds in the name of the House of Lords is the responsibility of each and every member above the age of 21. The lay membership of the House of Lords cannot escape their responsibility for the present condition of our law, and they cannot escape their responsibility for the present constitutional conditions. These are beyond the competence of the professional lawyer, who by training is bound to acknowledge the authority of Parliament without questioning as to how this authority is exercised.

The lay membership of the House of Lords have, however, the advantage that they are a constituent part of Parliament who can claim and require the advice and guidance of all the judges and bring this wider influence into our legal and constitutional affairs. In the lay membership of the House of Lords now lies the only possible safeguard for the constitutional rights and liberties of the subject, which the doctrine of Parliamentary sovereignty has so completely undermined. If the lay membership of the House of Lords can be active in this cause, they would take the first step in restoring the credit and standing of their House as an independent co-ordinate institution of Parliament and complete the conditions necessary for the re-establishment of the absolute supremacy of Parliament.

If we have any doubt as to the fundamental soundness of English principles of law and government, we need not only study our own history but study the strength and resilience of modern democracy of the American Union based upon English Common Law and expressed in their Declaration of Independence:-

> "We hold these truths to be self evident that all men are created equal, that they are endowed by their Creator with certain unalienable rights, that among these are life, liberty and the pursuit of happiness. That to secure these rights, governments are instituted among men, deriving their just powers from the consent of the governed. That whenever any form of government becomes destructive of these ends, it is the right of the people to alter or abolish it and to institute new government laying its foundation on such principles and organizing its powers in such form as to them shall seem most likely to effect their safety and happiness."

There are indeed features in American public life which may not be attractive. These features, however, are the corruption of American polity due to the attempt to compromise with French revolutionary ideology with its brutal materialism and its mock political democracy of the party system. In addition, the American constitution has all the weaknesses of an artificial creation. Nevertheless, these factors cannot disguise but rather add to the basic strength of the American political system and by which they have replaced the British Political and industrial leadership of the world.

The Americans themselves see the national strength and vigour as springing from their law and their constitution founded on that law. That law is English law. In the Declaration of Independence, the founders of American democracy refer to the free system of English Laws and the Common Law of England, and its basic concepts remain the foundation of American democracy. After a century and a half of political separation, Professor Lowell of Harvard records the fact that English decisions have never ceased to be cited in America. On the other hand, we in England have given the deepest considerations to American decisions. As recently as 1939, an English Parliamentary report dealing with certain aspects of the Bill of Rights, which had not come up for legal decision in England, cited cases from the Supreme Court of Massachusets and the Supreme Court of the United States, as guides to an English interpretation.

In the Constitution of the State of Maryland, English Common Law rights which are in England are lost, are specifically guaranteed by Article 5 of the Declaration of Rights, which reads:-

> "...the inhabitants of Maryland are entitled to the Common Law of England and the trial by jury according to the course of that law, and the benefit of such of the English statutes as existed on the fourth of July, 1776."

In America, these foundations in English Law have not been lost by any theory of sovereignty. Dean Roscoe Pound, in his "Spirit of the Common Law", directly associates the American law and government with English law and government when he wrote:-

> "Toward King, legislature and plurality of the electorate the Common Law has taken the same attitude. Within the limits in which the law recognises them as supreme it has but to obey them. But it reminds them that they rule under God and the law. And when fundamental law sets limits to their authority or bids them to proceed in a definite path, the Common Law courts have consistently refused to give effect to their acts beyond these limits. Juristically, this attitude of the Common Law courts, which we call the doctrine of the supremacy of the law, has its basis in the feudal idea of the relation of king and subject and the reciprocal rights and duties involved therein. Historically it goes back to the fundamental notions of Germanic Law. Philosophically, it is a doctrine that the sovereign and all agents thereof are bound to act upon principles, and not according to arbitrary will; are obliged to conform to reason, instead of being free to follow caprice. Along with the doctrine of judicial precedent and trial by jury, this doctrine of the supremacy of the law is one of the three distinctively characteristic institutions of the Anglo-American legal system.
>
> (page 64)

These concepts cannot be reconciled with either Austinian sovereignty or with French Revolutionary ideology, the rejection of which is more specifically emphasised in the Bill of Rights or Declaration of Rights of some of the States which declare:-

> "Absolute arbitrary power over the lives, liberty and property of freemen exists nowhere in a republic, not even in the largest majority."

The American constitution, like that of England, was never intended for political party operation, and the idea of party politics was repugnant to the founders of American democracy. This is clear from the words of George Washington in his first inaugural address as the first President of the United States of America. He then declared:-

> "The very idea of the power and the rights of the people to establish government presupposes the duty of every individual to obey the established government. All obstructions to the execution of the laws, all combinations and associations under whatever plausible character, with the real design to direct, control, counteract, or sway the regular deliberation and action of the constituted authorities are destructive of the fundamental principle and of fatal tendency. They serve to organise faction, to give it an artificial and extraordinary force, to put in the delegated will of the nation the will of a party, often a small but artful and enterprising minority of the community; and according to the alternate triumph of different parties, to make the administration the mirror of the ill-conceived and incongruous projects of faction, rather than the organ of consistent and wholesome plans digested by common councils, and modified national interest. However, combinations and associations of the above descriptions may now and then answer popular ends, they are likely in the course of time and things to become potent engines by which cunning, ambitious and unprincipled men will be enabled to subvert the

power of the people, and to usurp for themselves the reins of government, destroying afterwards the very engines which have lifted them to unjust dominion."

Washington's successor, John Adams, in his first inaugural address as President, repeated the same warning:-

"We should be unfaithful to ourselves if we should ever lose sight of the danger to our liberties - if anything partial or extraneous should infect the purity of our free, fair, virtuous and independent elections. If any election is to be determined by a majority of a single vote, and that can be procured by a party through artifice or corruption, the government may be the choice of a party for its own ends, not for the nation for the national good."

Under the influence of French Revolutionary ideology, the American party system has been allowed to corrupt and obliterate these concepts of free government, mainly in the local government field but more markedly in the fillings of the office of the Chief Executive in which the members of the Electoral College are bound by oath to void the purpose of the Constitution and to adhere to strictly party nomination. Even so, the American people have never unconditionally surrendered their power into the control of the party system as we have in England. The Americans have to a great extent, made the party organisation subject to law which in most states not only governs their public acts but also their internal organisation. These laws oblige the political parties to conduct their affairs along prescribed lines where organisations and the appointment of delegates to party conventions are concerned, and the choice of party candidates for election is conducted by the State in primary elections on lines as strict as the elections themselves. Whether this public control of the party organisation has proved adequate to overcome the anti-democratic tendencies of political parties, is a question which only the Americans themselves must answer. It is obvious, however, that the vital principle that all public authority, including that of party organisation, is subject to law has been recognised.

The American Courts of Law, by enforcing the law of the constitution, effectively prevent any political party, however powerful, from altering the structure of the State of the Federal Union. The American Constitution is subject to amendment and change but only by a process outside the control of any political party.

Apart from the Chief Executive, government office in America is not a party preserve and does not provide a political career to the elected representatives of the people in their capacity as legislators. American democracy has upheld the principles of our own Revolutionary settlement as laid down in the English Bill of Rights and Act of Settlement, preserving the principle of the purity and independence of popular representation by not allowing any elected representative the benefit of federal or state office or patronage. The American Cabinet is, in fact, the Presidential Privy Council, consisting not exclusively of professional party politicians but of men and women chosen by the President (subject to Senate approval) who, in other walks of life, have established their ability and capacity for office and administration. The President's choice is nationwide, not excluding the Civil Service but excluding all elected members of Congress.

There is, further, the provision that all legislation and public acts are subject to review by the Courts of Law, in actions at law. This means that no acts of legislation or administration can retain their validity once their enforcement has been declared as unconstitutional. Here we have an example of the immense power of juristic reasoning whereby courts of law armed with no weapons of enforcement can impose their judgements even on the executive authority armed with all the power of the state.

The fact is that the Americans have found no difficulty in reconciling their democracy with the juristic process of our Common Law. As Dicey himself said in his "Law of the Constitution":-

> "The power... of the courts which maintains the process of the constitution as the law of the land and thereby keeps each authority within its proper sphere is exerted with an ease and regularity which has astounded and perplexed constitutional critics. The explanation is that while the judges of the United States control the actions of the Constitution, they nevertheless perform purely judicial functions since they never decide anything but the case before them."

(Law of the Constitution, A.V.Dicey, 8th edit., p.159)

The Americans have made the rule of law by the Judiciary more marked than we have had to do in England in respect of Parliamentary legislation. In England, the House of Lords is our supreme Court, a co-ordinate institution of Parliament, whose consent was essential for all legislative purposes. The House of Lords had the benefit of the advice and guidance of all the judges.

In England, the constitutional validity of any legislation could be assumed, and the more cumbersome process of an action at law was not required to preserve our Parliamentary constitution through the centuries. In any case, this dependence upon the judiciary has in no way diminished the quality of political and civil freedom of American democracy. This freedom based upon the legal democracy of English Common Law principles was the key to English achievement in the past and is the basis of American achievement in the present.

After a century and a half of contemptuous neglect, we in England are beginning to envy the Americans their political stability. Professor Denis W. Brogan, when he first examined the American Constitution, spoke of it as a Frankenstein monster and stated that it beggared credulity that the Americans base their political life on the cannons of the 18th century. He wrote:-

> "With what complexity of machinery are so many necessary things done, with what almost impassable barriers is the popular will at times confronted, with what self-satisfaction does the average American pride himself alike on his liberty and on his docility under constitutional restraint."
>
> (The American Political System, D. W. Brogan, Hamish Hamilton, 1933, p. 36)

Professor Brogan subsequently reached a different conclusion. Writing in the preface of the same work some fifteen years later, he had to acknowledge that:-

> "...the constitutional system so uncritically worshipped must have been on the whole a success. It has survived, it has been admired and almost or quite worshipped

by those whom it has affected. And the 'people' of the United States, under the Constitution and through the political system of which the Constitution is the core, have waxed strong and prosperous, have defended their own independence and security, and have profoundly affected the history of the world. This is the basic fact about the American political system, it has neither degenerated into tyranny or anarchy; it has unified an area the size of Europe not merely formally but spiritually."

(Revised Preface, 1947, p. V)

These words refer to principles of government which have prevailed in England since the dawn of English history, and by which England established herself as the most influential nation in the development of Western civilisation. The same principles of government established in America, though seriously marred by the corrupting power of French Revolutionary ideology, has nevertheless exalted a heterogeneous people drawn largely from the varied races of the world into a great power both politically and economically as the most stable democracy of all times; a democracy based upon the rule of law, the rule of English law.

The restoration of the rule of law in England raises an issue which can only be resolved in Parliament and, in particular, by the House of Commons. It cannot be raised in the Courts because the Courts are subordinate to Parliament, and it is not open to them to enquire into the nature of parliamentary authority, as long as that authority is expressed in a parliamentary manner, however, corrupted. It is, therefore, a matter for the people in the election of members to the House of Commons, because by only the free action of the people of England (or Britain) can the present lawless stranglehold of party in the House of Commons be terminated.

The power of the party system rests upon its control of the national patronage by which the managers of the party system have been able to convert popular representation into the stepping stones of personal ambition in the service of party interest.

National patronage is intended for national ends. When it was vested in the prerogative of the Crown as the constitutional fountain of honour and in the appointment to office it had to be exercised under the supervision of the independent House of Commons, over which the Crown had constitutionally no control. It is now exercised by the party managers for party purposes under no independent supervision and control and represents a monstrous corruption of the principle of Parliamentary representation.

In England, this principle can immediately be restored by the re-adoption of the two repealed clauses in the Act of Settlement. The first of these clauses reads:-

> "All matters and things relating to the well governing of this kingdom which are properly recognisable in the Privy Council by the laws and customs of this realm shall be transacted there and all resolutions taken thereupon shall be signed by such of the Privy Council as shall advise and consent to the same."

> (The Statutes Revised, 2nd edit., Vol 1, Act of Settlement, p. 761)

The other clause reads:-

> "That no person who has an office or place of profit under the King or receives a pension from the crown shall be capable of serving as a member of the House of Commons."

> (Ibid)

The restoration of these two clauses in the Act of Settlement would replace the secret and irresponsible Party Cabinet with what is still the legal executive authority of the Privy Council on principles of personal responsibility to Parliament. They would restore the pure representative principles to the House of Commons. It is not to be expected that these clauses would be re-enacted under the present dispensation, but it is open to the people of this country to make them effective without legislation.

This can be achieved by the election of Independent Members of the House of Commons, who in their elections are pledged to the following points:-

(1) To uphold the prerogatives of the Crown, the privileges of Parliament and the rights and liberties of the subject as by law established.

(2) To accept no post or office in government or administration.

(3) To refuse to give any vote of confidence to any minister unless appointed by the free exercise of the prerogative of the Crown and then only if such appointment commands his independent confidence.

(4) To act on his own independent judgement in all matters arising in Parliament and to follow in all matters the dictates of his conscience to the good of the nation and its free parliamentary Constitution.

With one third of the membership of the House of Commons so pledged no single party could then control the majority of the House of Commons, and party government on its present pretensions would be rendered impossible. The free exercise of the royal prerogative to appointments to office and honour would then be restored with the constitutional authority of the Privy Council, responsible to an independent and free Parliament. The executive authority would thus be placed on a national and not on a partisan basis.

Freed from the party stranglehold, Parliament can then become again the great organ of national authority and the custodian of the rights and liberties of the free born British, and could act again as the national tribunal in which every shade of opinion and every grievance can find lawful and constitutional expression. By restoring Parliament onto its legal basis, it could then be reformed and remoulded by lawful process to meet the requirements of our modern age.

As Burke expressed it in his address to the British Colonies in North America:-

> "As long as the solid and well disposed forms of this constitution remain, there is ever within Parliament itself a power of renovating its principles and effecting

a self-reformation, which no other plan of government has ever contained. This constitution has therefore admitted innumerable improvements either for the correction of the original scheme, or for removing corruptions, or for bringing its principles better to suit these changes which have successively happened in the circumstances of the nation."

(The Works of Edmund Burke, The World Classics CXIII, Vol. 5, p. 373)

The Historic issue which now faces our generations is one of law against lawlessness. Government by law must ever remain one of the highest aspiration of all human associations. Without law, government can be one of the most brutal forces from which man can suffer, being in the long run destructive of national welfare by its inevitable corruption of supreme executive authority.

With the crown in full exercise of its legal prerogatives, the present barriers in our public life can be broken down. The crown will then be able to command to responsible public service, the outstanding ability and capacity of our people, not excluding the great professional servants of the state. Such was the Privy Council as the executive authority of the English nation in the days of her greatness and glory.

We in Britain are the inheritors of the greatest system of law and government in the civilized world. We have the knowledge and experience by which our modern civilisation can be led back from the dark confusion in which it has lost itself. We have the capacity and the leadership for this high and noble endeavour. All we lack is the means whereby such leaders may be called to the highest levels of national service. Leadership is a product of character and capacity, and that is our crying need in all our national activities to-day. We need above all to re-establish the great values of our national inheritance, in the supremacy of our greatest national institution, the high and most honourable court of Parliament. Thus, we shall protect our rights as free born Britons, enshrined in Magna Carta and accorded to us in our great Common Law. Then, indeed, can Britain lead the world (*by example**) because Britons will then be able to lead themselves. The long proven and hard-tested principles of English Law and Government remain the only hopeful basis of achieving the enduring and stable foundation of human association and an ordered world.

    * editorial comment

APPENDIX

AUSTIN AND DICEY'S DOCTRINE OF PARLIAMENTARY SOVEREIGNTY

T he constitutional basis of Parliamentary Government, based upon the Party Cabinet system, rests upon A. V. Dicey's "Law of the Constitution", in which he applied John Austin's theory of sovereignty to the English Parliament. For this, he had no historic, constitutional or legal authority whatsoever in that the doctrine abolishes all constitutional law. What is even more remarkable is that John Austin himself repudiated the application of his theory of sovereignty to the English Parliament.

Austin though rejecting the free concepts of English Common Law, nevertheless had a passionate attachment to the English Parliamentary constitution which was the product of that law. In 1860 before he died, Austin published his "Plea for the Constitution", which concluded with this declaration:-

> "Our own common attachment to our positive constitution is the strongest bond to our happy political union. This constitution has been ameliorated during long succession of ages and changes, whilst European government of kindred origin and form died of decay and violence before they could arrive at maturity. Frequent reforms of this Constitution, not commanded by manifest necessity, must destroy or impair the veneration with which we yet regard it, and should this bond of union be thus lightly dissolved, we shall probably pass through the evils brought on the people of France by fierce dissensions and political scepticism."

Austin was fully aware that this theory of sovereignty though "universally true without exception", could not be applied to the supreme legislatures of Common Law countries such as the English Parliament or legislatures in the American Union, but that sovereignty lay elsewhere. In other words, Austin's theory of sovereignty is nothing more than an academic exercise with no practical implications where Common Law countries are concerned. Austin recognised the fact that in Common Law countries, the people have never, in fact or in fiction, conditionally or unconditionally, by conquest or by grant, surrendered their rights or liberties. The people, therefore, are legally an essential element of the sovereign power. As Austin put it in his lectures on Jurisprudence:-

> "In our country for example one component part of the sovereign or supreme body is the numerous body of the Commons (in the strict signification of the name) that is to say such of the Commons (in the largest acceptation of the term) as share the sovereignty with the King and the Peers and elect the members of the Commons House."

> (Provence of Jurisprudence Determined, 2nd Edit., Vol. 1, p. 201)

The people have thus not surrendered their sovereignty to their elected representatives whose position is, therefore, limited to that of trustees for the people on terms which have been determined by what Austin called "exterior" and "Supreme" legislature of which the people as a whole form an essential part. These terms are what we would call fundamental or constitutional law.

In the case of the English Parliament, the fundamental law is that the legislative supremacy of Parliament is that of, what Austin called, a tripartite authority which is supreme only by the co-ordination of its three institutions of Kings, Lords and Commons. This tripartite condition of parliamentary supremacy is a fundamental law which has been affirmed by Austin to be a bar to any application of his theory of sovereignty to Parliament.

Austin wrote:-

> "Adopting the language of most of the writers who have treated of the British Constitution; I commonly suppose that ...Parliament...is possessed of the sovereignty; or I

commonly suppose that the King and the Lords, with the members of the Commons House, form a tripartite body which is sovereign or supreme. But speaking accurately the members of the Commons House are merely trustees for the body by which they are elected and appointed; and consequently the sovereignty always lies with the King, and the Peers with the electoral body of the Commons. That a trust is imposed by the party delegating and the party representing engages to discharge that trust, seems to be imported by the correlative expression delegation and representation. It were absurd to suppose that delegating empowers the representative party to defeat or abandon any of the purposes for which the latter is appointed..."

(Province of Jurisprudence Determined, 2nd edit., p. 203.)

Austin here clearly warns that a sovereign Parliament can defeat or abandon the purpose for which it exists.

Austin insists that the people are superior to the elected representatives and constitute a superior legislature which controls the ordinary legislature. He wrote:-

"A law of the Parliament, or a law of the Commons House which affected to abrogate a law of the extraordinary and ulterior legislature would not be obeyed by the Courts of Justice. The tribunals would enforce the latter in the teeth of the former. They would examine the competence of the ordinary legislature to make the abrogating law, as they would examine the competence of any subordinate corporation to establish a by-law or other statute or ordinance. In the State of New York, the ordinary legislature is controlled by the extraordinary legislature in the manner I have described. The body of citizens appointing the ordinary legislature forms an extraordinary and ulterior legislature by which the constitution of the state was directly established; and any law of the ordinary legislature which conflicts with constitutional law directly proceeding from the extraordinary legislature would be treated by the courts of justice as a legally invalid act. That such an extraordinary and ulterior legislature is a good and useful institution I pretend not to affirm. I merely affirm that the institute is possible, that in one political society the institution actually obtains."

(2nd edit., p. 205)

Austin has thus at least harmonised his theory with the conditions of Common Law constitutions.

Any claim that Parliamentary sovereignty is derived from Austinian theory falsifies Austin's own political position. Yet it is on such falsification that the basis of our own modern political system is based. For example, in Eastwood and Keeton's "The Austinian Theories of Law and Sovereignty", we have the following passage:-

"Every law, then, is a command which obliges to a course of external conduct. The next question to be discussed is what is the source of the command? By whom is it issued and enforced? In Austin's view it is issued and enforced by the sovereign and by the sovereign he meant such a body as the Parliament of Great Britain. A law in England is according to Austin a command issued by the joint action of King, the House of Lords, the House of Commons and addressed to the people. He thus has given the impression to some people that the sovereign is external to the community and that law is the arbitrary creation of the ruling body."

(Page 30)

Thus, where Austin was sound on the constitutional and historical applications of his theory to Common Law legislature, Dicey rejected Austin's argument on the ground that he had no understanding of the English Constitution or the meaning of Parliamentary supremacy. Dicey, for example, declared:-

"Nothing is more certain than that no English judge ever conceded or, under the present constitution, can concede that Parliament is in any legal sense a "trustee" for the electors; of such a feigned trust the courts know nothing."

(10th edit., p. 75)

As a constitutional authority, Dicey must have known that the liberty of the subject had ever been very much a matter for the courts before Parliamentary supremacy was superceded by his doctrine of Parliamentary sovereignty. Further, he must have known also that under Parliamentary supremacy the possibility of Parliament legislating in terms which infringed the liberty of the subject and which were beyond the competence of the courts to challenge was reduced to the very minimum under considerable legal safeguards of which the supremacy of Parliament resting on the co-ordination of three independent institutions expressed in a written form was the most potent. Further in the legal condition of Parliamentary supremacy, the supreme court of English law, whose decisions were binding on the lower courts, was the lay membership of the House of Lords, and the House of Lords in its dual capacity as a co-ordinate institution of Parliament and as the supreme court, did most emphatically recognise the principle of legal trusteeship on which Austin insisted. Further, the House of Lords had the advice of the whole bench of judges who, in this capacity, would most certainly have reminded the House of Lords of this position of trust in matters affecting the liberty of the subject. Unlike the position in the United States, where the constitutional validity of legislation can only be determined by an action at law, in England, it could be safely presumed that all acts of Parliament and all judgements of the House of Lords would not conflict with but would conform to the fundamental law of which the outstanding symbol is Magna Carta which in Austin's expression had been established by the superior legislature.

Dicey, however, agrees that Austinian sovereignty is not applicable to the American Union but not for the reasons which Austin put forward but solely on the grounds that the American constitution covers a federal state, whereas the English constitution covers what he called a unitary state. In other words, the application of a universal truth without exception is true only if the structure of the state permits it!

Dicey, in the "Law and the Constitution", tells us:-

> "A federal state derives its existence from the Constitution just as a corporation derives its existence from the grant by which it is created. Hence every power, executive, legislative or judicial whether it belong to the nation or to the individual states is subordinate and controlled by the constitution... This doctrine of the supremacy of the Constitution is familiar to every American, but in England even trained lawyers find difficulty in following it out to its legitimate consequences. The difficulty arises from the fact that under the English Constitution no principle is recognised which bears any resemblance to the doctrine (essential to Federalism) that the Constitution constitutes the "Supreme Law of the Land". In England we have laws which may be called fundamental or constitutional because they deal with important principles...lying at the basis of our institutions. But with us there is no such thing as a supreme law or law which tests the validity of other laws."

(10th edit., p. 144)

But what grounds are there, apart from Dicey's own special doctrine of parliamentary sovereignty, to suggest that a unitary state is not equally bound by constitutional law as is a federal state? Dicey, in the "Law of the Constitution", tells us that:-

> "The foundations of a Federal State are a complicated contract. This contract contains a variety of terms which have been agreed to and generally after mature deliberation by the states which make up the confederacy. To base an arrangement on this kind upon understandings and conventions would be certain to generate misunderstandings and disagreements. The Articles of the Treaty or, in other words, of the Constitution must therefore be a written document of which the terms are open to no misapprehension."

(10th edit., p. 146)

It is not necessary to raise the question here whether any constitution is not a "complicated contract" which contains a variety of terms. Nor is it necessary to affirm the historic and recognised fact that Magna Carta constitutes the fundamental law of the English Constitution. It is only necessary to show that the English constitution is bound by a fundamental law on the same basis as is the American federal state, for Dicey's doctrine of the sovereignty of the parliament to fall to the ground and that therefore on this score alone, Dicey's elaborate distinction between federalism and unitarianism must be regarded as nonsense.

At the time Dicey was propounding his thesis, England was, and still is, as much part of a composite state as any state in the American Union. England is part of the United Kingdom of Great Britain which was brought into existence by a Treaty of Union between two independent Kingdoms of England and Scotland. Dicey would invite us to believe that if England and Scotland had formed a federal union, as was suggested at the time of the treaty, the Treaty would have constituted fundamental law to which a federated kingdom would have been subject. As, however, these nations formed a political though not a legal or ecclesiastical unitary state, the solemn Treaty of Union has no more fundamental quality than some minor Dentist Act of 1878. It is necessary to consider Dicey's words in which he supports this astounding constitutional proposition. He wrote:-

> "There are indeed important statutes such as the Act embodying the Treaty of Union with Scotland, with which it would be political madness to tamper gratuitously; there are utterly unimportant statutes such, for example, as the Dentist Act of 1878, which may be repealed or modified at the pleasure or caprice of Parliament; but neither the Act of Union with Scotland nor the Dentist Act of 1878 has more claim than the other to be considered a supreme law. Each embodies the will of the sovereign legislative power, and each can be legally altered or repealed by Parliament; neither tests the validity of the other."

(Law of the Constitution, 10th edit., p. 145)

This passage was more fully developed when Dicey, in association with R. S. Rait, produced their joint study entitled "Thoughts on the Scottish Union" in which the authors tell us:-

> "The statesmen of 1707, though giving full sovereign power to the Parliament of Great Britain, clearly believed in the possibility of creating an absolutely sovereign legislature which should yet be bound by unalterable laws. From one point of view, which is clearly recognised by most modern jurists, the attempt to limit absolutely sovereign power involves something like a contradiction of ideas. For a true sovereign, whether called Emperor, King or Parliament, who can change every law, can also change the very law which limits his authority."

(Page 252)

If we examine the Treaty of Union between England and Scotland, nowhere do we find a single reference or even the slightest suggestion, that the Parliament of Great Britain is to be an "absolutely sovereign legislature". On the contrary, implicit in the whole treaty is the conception, not of a sovereign, but of a supreme Parliament bound by fundamental law of which the treaty itself would be a part. To give but one of the many possible examples, Article XXV of the Treaty of Union, as confirmed and ratified by the Parliaments of England and Scotland, and standing as law, declares:-

> "It is hereby statute and ordained that this Act of Parliament with the establishment therein confirmed shall be held and observed in all time coming as a fundamental and essential condition of any treaty of union to be concluded between the two Kingdoms without alteration thereof or derogation thereto in any sort for ever."

In what way does this differ from the processes and conditions governing the setting up of a federal union which Dicey says constitutes fundamental law but, in this case of a unitary state, has no more legal significance than a Dentist Act? The existence of a Treaty of Union to set up a state to be known as the United Kingdom of Great Britain is surely as much a constituent act as the ratification of the United States of America, and must have an equal binding force. If this is so, then Parliament is no more sovereign than the legislatures in the American Union. Only in one instance can it be said that by British Legislation has the Treaty of Union been directly violated, and that was when patronage was imposed upon the Church of Scotland. This involved an infringement of the Revolutionary settlement to the Scots as important as the freedom of election is to the English and is the equivalent of a restoration of the nomination boroughs as they existed before the Reform Act of 1832. The Treaty of Union protected this settlement, and its violation was an act of bad faith which has caused endless misery, disorganisation and disruption to the Scottish people. If the Court of Session had been a court of Common Law, there can be no doubt whatever that this act of British legislation would have been declared ultra vires , as Lord Campbell, an English judge, later suggested. This one act of Parliament can hardly be accepted as evidence of a sovereign power in relation to the Act of Union. It is, however, impressive as evidence that acts of legislative sovereignty are bad in faith, lawless in their consequences and will, in the end, destroy and disrupt a unitary state no less than one with a federal structure as well as an empire, however powerful.

Only on such grounds of bad faith can Dicey support his contention that the English Constitution differs from the American in being free from all constitutional or fundamental law.

It is to be remarked that though Dicey lays it down as a general proposition that Federal States are bound by constitutional law enforced and upheld by the judicial process, he, in fact, relies only on Common Law America for his example. He mentions it is true, the Swiss Confederation and the German Empire, both civil law countries who do not, in any case, recognise a fundamental or constitutional law which the sovereign power cannot alter or disregard. Of the Swiss Confederation, he tells us their statesmen have failed in keeping the judicial apart from the executive department, and this failure constituted a serious flaw in the Swiss constitution. As far as the German Empire is concerned, he dismisses it as too full of anomalies to be taken as a representative example.

The judicial basis, is not therefore, a fundamental condition of a Federal State, and it must therefore be taken that it exists in America, not because America is a Federal State but because her constitution is founded on Common Law principles, the same principles which have maintained the English Constitution through the centuries. If we substitute "Common Law" for the word "Federalism", we can gauge in Dicey's own words what this common law principle means in constitutional matters when he writes:-

> "Federalism substitutes litigation for legislation and none but a law fearing people will be inclined to regard the decisions of a suit as equivalent to the enactment of a law. The main reason why the United States has carried out the federal system with unequalled success is that the people of the Union are more thoroughly imbued with legal ideas than any other existing nation. Constitutional questions ...are of daily occurrence and constantly occupy the Courts...This acquiescence or submission is due to the American inheriting the legal notions of Common Law, i.e., of the most legal system of law' (if the expression may be allowed) in the world."

> (Law of the Constitution, 10th edit., p. 179)

This inheritance is derived from England. The Americans themselves have no doubt whatever on this matter. On this very passage from Dicey, Professor McIlwain of Harvard was inspired to write his essay "The High Court of Parliament and its Supremacy" in the introduction to which he wrote:-

> "If Professor Dicey had confined his statement to Federations in English speaking countries, it would be true, but true because the countries are English speaking and not because they are organised under a Federal system. In short the idea of a judicial review of legislation and of a constituent law as well are, in origin, English ideas and arise in no way from Federalism itself. Their source is to be sought in English history rather than in the conditions of modern political life."

> (page 6)

The conditions of modern political life in England spring directly from the application by Dicey of the constitutional lawlessness of Austinian sovereignty in place of the legal notions of the Common Law - the most legal system of law in the world, as Dicey said, which the Americans have retained as the basis of their own democracy.

THE END

BIBLIOGRAPHY

Adams, G. B. *Origin of the English Constitution* (Yale University Press, 1912)

Allen, C. K. *Law in the Making* (Clarendon Press, 1927)

Allen, C. K. *Law and Orders* (Stevens and Sons, 1945)

Amery, L. S. *Thoughts on the Constitution* (Geoffrey Cumberlege Oxford University Press, 1947)

Atlee, C. R. et al. *Problems of a Socialist Government* (Gollancz, 1933)

Austin, J. *The Province of Jurisprudence determined* (J. Murray, 1832)

Bagehot, W. *The English Constitution* (Chapman & Hall, 1867)

Benn, A.W. *Article.* (Daily Express, 20th November 1969)

Blackstone, W. *Commentaries on the Laws of England* (Clarendon Press, 1765)

Brogan, D. W. *The American Political System* (Hamish Hamilton, 1933)

Brougham, H. *The British Constitution* (Charles Knight, 1844)

Bryce, J. *Studies in History and Jurisprudence* (Clarendon Press, 1901)

Bryce, J. Preface. *Democracy and the Organisation of Political Parties* by M. Ostrogorski (Macmillan & Company, 1902)

Buckland, W. W. & McNair, A. D. *Roman Law and Common Law* (Cambridge University Press, 1936)

Buckle, G. E.; Monypenny, W. F. *Life of Benjamin Disraeli* (John Murray, 1910)

Burke, E. *A Vindication of Natural Society* (M. Cooper, 1756)

Burke, E. *Thoughts on the Cause of the Present Discontents* (Unknown, 1770)

Burke, E. *Select Works of Edmund Burke vol 2* (Oxford University Press, 1918)

Churchill, W. *The Gathering Storm* (Houghton Mifflin, 1948)

Clynes, J. R. *Article* (Manchester Guardian, 16th September 1951)

Cooper, D. *Talleyrand* (Arrow Books, 1932)

Cowper, W. *The Task* (Joseph Johnson 1785)

Creasy, E. S. *The Rise and Progress of the English Constitution* (Richard Bentley, 1853)

Cripps, S. Lecture. *Where stands Socialism Today* (Fabian Summer School, 1932)

Crossman, R. H. S. Introduction. *The English Constitution* by Walter Bagehot (Fontana Library, 1963)

Denning, A. T. *The Changing Law* (Stevens & Sons Ltd.,1953)

Denning, F. T. Romanes Lecture. *From Precedent to Precedent* (Clarendon Press, 1959)

Dicey, A. V. *Introduction to the Study of the Law of the Constitution* (Macmillan & Co. Ltd, 1885)

Dicey, A. V. Arnold Essay. *The Privy Council* (Macmillan & Co. Ltd, 1887)

Dicey, A. V. *Lectures on the Relations between Law and Public Opinion in England during the 19th Century* (Macmillan & Co. Ltd., 1916)

Dicey, A. V.; Rait, R. S. *Thoughts on the Union between England & Scotland* (Macmillan & Co., 1920)

Eastwood, R. A.; Keeton, G. W. *The Austinian Theories of Law and Sovereignty* (Methuen & Co. Ltd., 1929)

Fifoot, C. H. S. *English Law and its Background* (G. Bell & Sons, 1932)

Fifoot, C. H. S. *Lord Mansfield* (Clarendon Press, 1936)

Figgis, J. N. *Political Thought from Gerson to Grotius* (Cambridge University Press, 1907)

Fitzroy, A. W. *The History of the Privy Council* (J. Murray, 1928)

Fortescue, J. *De Laudibus Legum Angliae* (unknown, circa 1543)

Fox, C. J. *Debate* HofC Hansard VOL. 24 Col. 736 8th March 1784

Garvin, J. L. *The Life of Joseph Chamberlain* (Macmillan & Co. Ltd, 1933)

George, L. *Testimony. Procedure in Public Business* Parliamentary Select Committee, 1931

Gierke, O. *Political Theories of the Middle Ages* (Cambridge University Press, 1900)

Gough, J. W. *Fundamental Law in English Constitutional History* (The Clarendon Press, 1955)

Greaves, H. R. G. *The British Constitution* (Allen & Unwin, 1938)

Holland, F. Continuation. *Constitutional History of England* by Thomas Erskine May (Longmans, 1912)

Hale, M. *The History of the Common Law in England* (Nut & Gosling, 1939)

Hallam, H. *View of the State of Europe in the Middle Ages* (John Murray, 1818)

Halsbury's *Laws of England* (Butterworths, 1907)

Hamson, C. J. Broadcast Talks. *Law Reform and Law Making* (Heffer, 1953)

Hart, H. L. A. Introduction. Library of Ideas Edition. *Province of Jurisprudence Determined* by John Austin (Weidenfield and Nicolson, 1954)

Haseltine. Preface. Chrimes Edition *'De Laudibus Regum Angliae'* by John Fortescue (Cambridge University Press, 1942)

Hatsell, J. *Precedent of Proceedings to the House of Commons* (H. Hughs, 1785)

Hewart, G. *The New Despotism* (Ernest Benn Ltd., 1929)

Hogg, Q. M. *Quote.* (The Sunday Times 1970)

Holt, J. Minority Judgement. *All the Proceedings in relation to the Aylesbury Men* House of Parliament. (Edward Jones 1705)

Hooker, R. *Of the Laws of ecclesiastical Polity* (Self Published, 1593)

Jennings, I. *The Law and the Constitution* (University of London Press, 1953)

Jennings, I. *Cabinet Government* (Cambridge University Press, 1936)

Keeton, G. W. *Elementary Principles of Jurisprudence* (Isaac Pitman & Sons, 1930)

Keeton, G. W. *The Passing of Parliament* (Ernest Benn Ltd., 1952)

Keith, A. B. *The British Cabinet System* (Stevens & Sons Ltd., 1939)

Keith, A. B. Commentary. *The Constitutional Law of England* by E. W. Ridges (Stevens and Sons Ltd., 1939)

Low, S. J. M. *The Governance of England* (T. Fisher Unwin, 1904)

Macaulay, T. B. *Essays on Hallam* (The Edinburgh Review, 1828)

Macaulay, T. B. *The History of England from the Accession of James II* (Longmans Green & Co. 1848)

Mackenzie, G. *Institutions of the Law in Scotland* (John Reid, 1684)

MacMillan, A. R. G. *The Evolution of the Scottish Judiciary* (W. Green, 1941)

MacMillan, H. *The Law and Other Things* (The Cambridge University Press, 1937)

MacMillan, H. *Quote.* The Times, 6th April 1948

Maine, H. S. *Popular Government* (John Murray, 1885)

Mallet de Pain, J. Mercure Briannique London Periodical 1798

Marriot, J. A. R. *English Political Institutions:* An Introductory Study (The Clarendon Press, 1913)

Massey, W. N. *A history of England during the Reign of George III* (J. W. Parker & Son, 1865)

McIlwain, C. H. *The Growth of Political Thought in the West* (The Macmillan Company, 1932)

Mckenzie, R. T. *British Political Parties* (William Heinemann, 1955)

Muir, R. *How Britain is Governed* (Constable & Co. Ltd., 1932)

Muir, R. Testimony. Select Committee. *Procedure on Public Business* (Commons Paper 1931)

Namier, L. B. *Conflicts: Studies in Contemporary History* (Macmillan & Co.,1942)

Namier, L. B. *Personalities and Powers* (Hamilton, 1955)

Ogg, D. *Ionnis Seldeni Ad Fletam Dissertatio* (Cambridge University Press, 1925)

Ostrogorski, M. *Democracy and the Organisation of Political Parties* (Macmillan, 1902)

Paley, W. *Principles of Moral and Political Philosophy* (R. Faulder, 1785)

Percy, E. Privy *Council under the Tudors* (Simpkin & Marshall, 1907)

Pound, D *The Spirit of the Common Law* (Marshall Jones Company, 1906)

Rait, R. S. *The Scottish Parliament before the Union of the Crowns* (Blackie and Son Ltd., 1901)

Rapin, P. *History of England* (James, John and Paul Knapton, 1732)

Rosebery. *Miscellanies Literary & Historical* (Hodder & Stoughton Ltd., 1921)

Smith, F. E. et al. *Rights of Citizenship* (F.Warne & Co., 1912)

Southey, R. *Epitaph on King John* (Morning Post, 28th May 1798)

Stephen, H. J. *New Commentaries on the Law of England* (Henry Butterworth, 1844)

Stephen, L. *The Science of Ethics* (Ballantyne Press, 1882)

Taswell-Langmead, T. P. *English Constitutional History* (Stevens & Haynes, 1875)

Tocqueville, A. de *The State of Society in France before the Revolution of 1789* (John Murray, 1888)

Trevelyan, G. M. *Introduction. Richard II* by Anthony Steel (Cambridge University Press, 1941)

Trevelyan, G. M. *An Autobiography and Other Essays* (Longmans, Green & Co., 1949)

Vinogradoff, P. *Roman Law in Medieval Europe* (Harper & brothers, 1909)

Wade, E.C. S. *Introduction. Introduction to the Study of the Law of the Constitution* 9th and 10th Edition (Macmillan and Company Ltd., 1939)

Printed by BoD™in Norderstedt, Germany